# When Writing with
# Technology
# Matters

# When Writing with Technology Matters

### Carol **Bedard** & Charles **Fuhrken**

## Stenhouse
P U B L I S H E R S

**www.stenhouse.com**

Portland, Maine

Stenhouse Publishers
www.stenhouse.com

Library of Congress Cataloging-in-Publication Data
Fuhrken, Charles, 1970-
  When writing with technology matters / Charles Fuhrken and Carol Bedard.
    pages cm
  Includes bibliographical references and index.
  ISBN 978-1-57110-937-8 (pbk. : alk. paper) -- ISBN 978-1-57110-987-3 (ebook : alk. paper) 1. Language arts--Computer-assisted instruction. 2. English language--Study and teaching--Computer-assisted instruction. 3. Educational technology. 4. Motion pictures in education. I. Bedard, Carol. II. Title.
  LB1576.7.F84 2013
    428.40785--dc23

                                                                    2012045135

Cover design, interior design, and typesetting by designboy creative group

Manufactured in the United States of America

PRINTED ON 30% PCW
RECYCLED PAPER

19 18 17 16 15 14 13   9 8 7 6 5 4 3 2 1

To
Roberta Raymond
and
Sheila Newell

# Contents

# Acknowledgments

When we were invited to participate in an integrated technology and language arts project, we saw learning that is expected in any literacy classroom—reading, writing, listening, speaking, researching, and so forth. But the students themselves told us and showed us that something more was happening. Something worth sharing.

We owe Roberta Raymond tremendous thanks for starting us on this path. She truly understands that if you give students the space to create, they will surprise and impress you with what they are capable of creating. We watched as her enthusiasm for letting learning happen became contagious.

Thanks also to the teachers of Houston Independent School District who welcomed us into their classrooms and the students who allowed us to work alongside them.

Sheila Newell's door was always open, and we would have gone every day to her classroom if we could have. Sheila reminded us that students are often their own best teachers. Thank you for sharing with us your students, who showed us what confidence and risk taking looks like in today's classrooms.

Our editor, Bill Varner, believed in our vision and helped shape the philosophical into the practical. We appreciated the support from the entire Stenhouse family along the way.

Thanks, finally, to our families, who could hardly wait for us to write the last sentence . . . which is this very one.

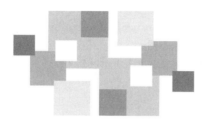

# Introduction

Texting on cell phones, listening to music on ipods, surfing the net on laptop computers, updating profiles on Facebook. Who are these people? They are the digital natives—young people who have been "plugged in" their entire lives. These are our students today—the twenty-first-century students who allowed us to pull up a chair, eavesdrop on their classroom conversations, chat with them, and learn *about* them . . . *from* them.

This is a book about writing. Specifically, it's a book about the settings that allow students to become invested—engrossed even—in writing. It's also about how our students today are wired to use technology as a tool in learning to become writers. Technology changes the writing process—and ultimately changes the writer. This is a book about writing and technology, because for the digital generation, they serve each other well.

## Technology's Place in the Literacy Classroom

Today a profound gap exists between the knowledge and skills most students learn in school and the knowledge and skills they need in typical twenty-first-century communities and workplaces (Partnership for 21st Century Skills 2011). This is precisely why creators of language arts curricula are no longer ignoring the fact that "our schools [must] teach our students how to use technology tools to solve problems, communicate, access information, and foster lifelong learning" (Cohen and Cowen 2008, 12). Leu (1997), more than a decade ago, warned, "Individuals unable to keep up with the information strategies generated by new information technologies will quickly be left behind" (65). In the twenty-first-century class-room, computers, networks, and multimedia are the necessary tools in addition to chalk, pen, and paper.

Technology has the capacity to allow for a broader vision of literacy instruction (Bruce 1997). Not only can students in the language arts classroom learn reading and writing, but a technologically infused curriculum can develop multiple essential literacies: technological literacy, visual literacy, informational literacy, and intertextuality (Smolin and Lawless 2003). Technological literacy is the ability to use computers and other technology to improve learning, productivity, and performance (Clinton 1997). Visual literacy is the ability to understand and produce visual messages (Avgerinou n.d.). Informational literacy refers to the ability to define, evaluate, analyze, and synthesize information (Smolin and Lawless 2003). Intertextuality represents the process of comprehending one text by means of a previously encountered text (Kristeva 1984). Conceptualizing literacy in these ways transforms the classroom from solely a text-based literate environment to one that embraces multiple literacies, and the richness that comes with a technological landscape is continually evolving.

## How This Book Is Organized

This book begins with ten reasons why writing with technology matters. We developed the reasons from the themes that emerged across two educational settings in which technology was seamlessly integrated into the literacy curricula.

We then provide glimpses into two literacy classrooms that integrated technology and language arts: Elementary students worked together on a filmmaking project and middle school students engaged in a cross-curriculum research project to produce a visual nonfiction essay. As we share with you what was happening and why, we will offer ideas for how technological tools can change writing instruction in your own classrooms.

Our conclusion looks across the two projects, spotlights the central ideas, and reveals what is possible when writing and technology are joined in ways that truly matter to students.

# Chapter 1
# Ten Reasons Why Writing with Technology Matters

Why does writing with technology matter? In our observations of two projects that integrated writing and technology in elementary and middle school classrooms, we found that, although the project activities the students engaged in were often different, the foundation and purpose of those activities united the projects. In this chapter, we provide an overview of the two projects and refer to aspects of them as we explore and explain why writing with technology matters in the classroom.

## Project 1: Reading and Writing to Launch Moviemaking

This moviemaking project for upper elementary students integrated technology into the language arts curriculum. The main components were:

- Reading: Students read popular chapter books and responded in literature circles and on a blog.
- Writing: Students wrote adaptations of chapter books. Supporting writing activities included posting responses on a blog, writing stories, conferring about their writing, creating Hollywood pitches to "sell" their stories, writing group stories, creating storyboards, and using scriptwriting software to format their stories as scripts.
- Moviemaking: Students assumed the roles of actors, costume and set designers, camera operators, directors, and producers. They used Windows Movie Maker and incorporated special effects.

## Project 2: Authoring the Visual Nonfiction Essay

This cross-curriculum project for middle school students focused on researching the time period from the Medieval to the Post-Renaissance. The main components were:

- Reading: Students read and annotated historical fiction books, participated in literature circles, and made note of possible topics for research.
- Researching: Students researched their cross-curriculum topics using both print and online sources.

- Writing: Students wrote across genres as they used their research to create independent projects. Students also created storyboards to plan collaborative essays.
- Videoing: Students collaboratively produced visual nonfiction essays; using Windows Movie Maker, they converted slides made in Microsoft PowerPoint to create a video replete with special effects.

With these two projects in mind, let's talk about the real possibilities that can exist when incorporating writing with technology.

# Why Writing with Technology Matters: The Ten Reasons

Why write with technology in the literacy classroom? Here are ten reasons that emerged in the two projects we observed.

## 1. Process matters.

By definition, a project is multistage or multistep, and project-based learning seeks to sustain students' motivation and thought for a sustained period of time so that they can understand the purposes, rationales, and connections of the steps toward the outcome or end products (Blumenfeld et al. 1991). In both projects, the integration of the language arts with technology informed these steps. That is, the intent of each project was to engage students in multiple and authentic aspects and levels of literary learning that ultimately combined and contributed to the students' goal of producing narrative and nonfiction videos.

It was moviemaking, not reading and writing, that was on the minds of elementary students as they began the integrated language arts–technology project. But students soon discovered that just like real Hollywood screenwriters, they had to first put the words on the page that could be turned into images on the big screen. Students began by reading chapter books—these books served as the basis of the story lines students developed through a number of writing activities, which included writing independently, conferring both face-to-face and online, writing collaboratively, and storyboarding. Throughout the process, the elementary students blogged about their daily activities and progress, their frustrations, and their successes, so the blog served as a record of their learning.

The middle school project also began with reading. Middle schooler Emelia offered, "Historical fiction can be educational but interesting at the same time." That was precisely why her teacher used historical fiction reading not only to engage students but also to provide exposure to some topics they could research.

The middle school research project required that students apply their research to projects they completed individually. Essentially, students were building a knowledge base at this stage that they could draw from later when they worked collaboratively on the visual nonfiction essay. Students realized that writing with technology presented challenges as well as capabilities that were not possible with paper and pen, and they grew as writers as a result of having to toggle between both print forms and visual forms as they synthesized their content into a cohesive whole. Therefore, reading, researching, writing independently, and writing collaboratively culminated in the students' ability to showcase their learning via the visual nonfiction essay.

In the projects, the *product* mattered, certainly, because it was a creation—a real, concrete representation of the students' efforts. But the *process* also mattered, and students became keenly aware that the product was made possible as a result of authentic stages of a complex process. And teachers became aware of what students learned by watching closely as students engaged in the process. Consequently, the products, although important, actually represented only a small part of the learning.

## 2. Engagement matters.

*Hard work* are the words that teachers and students involved in these projects used to describe what they were doing. So how is it that everyone was so willing to do so much hard work?

That's what *engagement* in the process allows. Students showed stick-to-itiveness because they were engaged in their work and viewed it as important (Hobbs 2007).

When the elementary students learned that they would be moviemakers, the excitement was palpable and audible. They knew what that meant—they could envision sitting in an auditorium crowded with family and friends, viewing a piece of work they had constructed. And when things got rough, students' desire to produce something great for others to see is what helped them push through. During filming, one student, Alonso, posted on the class blog, *We're practically all over the place doing tons of stuff. I only slept for, like, three hours and no more, because we have a ton of work to do.* Another student, Isaac, wrote, *I felt like I would finish by the time I was fifty.* Fortunately, all the elementary filmmaking groups reached deep to complete their movies for the premiere day. And on that final day, students were sure to take home DVDs of their movies because, as the teachers reported, they wanted to post them on YouTube.

The fact is, projects such as these allow for students to sustain their focus and attention and become invested in what they are doing. Middle school student Melissa found that constructing the visual part of the visual nonfiction essay meant constant tinkering with technology in order to achieve the desired effects. She said in an interview, *It takes a lot of time and patience. But you need that if [the project] is going to be good.*

Engagement allows for meaningful, enduring learning.

## 3. Critical thinking matters.

The projects allowed students opportunities to make decisions independently and col-laboratively and space to think critically and creatively when solving problems, which in turn allowed teachers insight into their students' capacities for critical thinking and meaning making when given environments that encouraged them (Swed 2001).

The nature of the projects allowed teachers to turn over the reins to the students, plac-ing them in the roles of decision makers through and through. When constructing their visual essay, for example, middle school students Adrian, Keith, and Patrick discussed and came to agreement on a number of matters including the central focus, the font size of text, the background color, the music, the mode of narration, the need for authentic images, and the reliability and accuracy of their sources, just to name a few.

Many of the decisions the students made required them to think critically about their own work. Middle school students Chad and Jerad wrestled with finding the precise wording to capture the feeling they wanted to convey. After writing *They [the monks] rushed out to meet their unexpected guests* in their visual essay draft, they decided to give the idea more effect by adding, *but their guests have sinister intentions.* This decision re-quired deeper, finer, specific thinking on the students' part—a level of thinking that is often not brought to daily assignments.

Many decisions the students made in these projects allowed them to tap into their creative thinking. Middle schooler Connor infused humor in his newspaper titled *The Sea of Trolls Chronicles* by including a joke section. Elementary student Gabriel re-created a televised press conference, complete with a running ticker tape.

Because the projects were designed so that the students were in charge of their own schedule, their own creations, and their own learning, they acquired many workplace skills including organization, decision making, and attention to detail. Ms. Garcia, a teacher in the elementary project, reflected in a group interview:

> I think they're shaped as workers. These are intelligent children, but this is the hardest they've had to work in their educational careers. It's a com-mitment they have to see from the start to the finish.

Critical thinking can occur when students are given the space to make important decisions on their own.

## 4. Research matters.

Research for the twenty-first-century learner involves gathering information from mul-tiple formats, including traditional and digital print, audio, photography, and video. It involves viewing and analyzing images—pictures and videos—and listening to music to consider what mood the tune and lyrics evoke. Today, because technology allows students to access a large amount of information almost instantaneously (Smolin and Lawless 2003), research has become embedded in all phases of the writing process.

As a group of elementary students was designing a set in preparation for filming a scene in their movie, they realized they wanted to include hieroglyphics on a painted backdrop. Without hesitation, one group member, Rose, went to the computer and within minutes had accessed the needed information. And middle schoolers Melissa and Jessica returned to their sources when they hit a snag and needed to verify a fact they had recorded in their notes but later questioned. "Let's check that" was a comment we often overheard as groups worked to construct their essays.

Research is no longer what students do for an hour in the library before the writing begins. Research now emerges organically and figures into many stages of the writing process; it is often the answer to students' inquiries.

## 5. Collaboration matters.

Collaboration has been named a twenty-first-century skill that students must acquire during their school experiences because it is a critical skill in the global marketplace (Partnership for 21st Century Skills 2011). Across the projects, we witnessed true, constructive collaboration in which multiple perspectives were offered and considered, aha moments abounded, and thinking was pushed and deepened as a result of the exchanges.

One collaborative arrangement for the elementary filmmakers was aided by technology because students responded and reflected on a class blog daily. The blog helped students form a community of learners that allowed them to gain access to the goings-on of other groups, give and receive status reports of their progress, and contribute to other groups' movies by providing suggestions. For example, when one student, Julie, posted that her group made guitars out of paper in order to film a scene, another student offered, *Why don't you use Guitar Hero guitars?* Another beneficial collaborative arrangement for these students included working with university students to improve their stories.

Collaboration was successful for the middle school students creating a visual nonfiction essay together because the students had conducted and applied their research individually before meeting together. Mrs. Newstead, a seventh-grade teacher, said in an interview, "Too often students are placed in groups too early, so they don't have anything to contribute." Because students entered their groups armed with a growing bank of knowledge on their topics, their discussions were focused, quickly paced, and meaningful. Furthermore, students seemed more willing to stay the course together when at an impasse rather than reach out to the teacher for assistance.

As you read about the two projects later in the book, ask yourself, "What would have been lost had students worked independently throughout the process?" One middle school student, Patrick, told us: "I learned that if you work as a team, the [product] will look better than if you worked on it by yourself." And an elementary student, Alonso, grimaced at the thought of going it solo, pondering how the quality of his group's movie would have been affected: "If we hadn't worked together, the whole story would have fallen apart. It could not have been done alone."

Collaboration pushes thinking and encourages sustained effort.

## 6. Audience matters.

Writing for a real audience matters because students often develop a passion for their writing when they know it has the potential to reach an audience outside the four walls of the classroom (Kajder 2010; Strassman and O'Connell 2007–2008).

Because those participating in the elementary moviemaking project knew that all movies would be shown to their peers and the larger community of family and friends, students' blog postings were replete with comments like *I'm getting nervous* and *We need to start filming!* as the premiere day approached. In the last week of filming and editing, students saw their hard work coming together into something worthy of being shared, but they also realized the value of schedules and meeting deadlines. In the final days, some groups were confident and issued challenges, such as *Let's see who makes the best movie.* Others had moments of weakness and expressed the pressure that was mounting: *Can you believe it's already this Friday when we have to present?* By premiere day, though, the groups had managed to put the finishing touches on their work and were present to experience what having a real audience looks and sounds like—a packed auditorium filled with giggles of joy and gasps of surprise and tremendous applause for the budding moviemakers.

For the middle school students, knowing that their essays would be viewed by peers as well as anonymous viewers who accessed them (such as on YouTube) meant that many groups spent a great deal of time selecting and refining their topics. One group chose the bubonic plague as the topic of their visual nonfiction essay because after researching the topic, they felt it was important to show *how widespread the plague was, and the preventions and remedies used in that time period.* One group member, Catherine, explained in an interview, *Our message was to show how the plague affected that time period and how different healthcare was then from how it is today.*

When students write with an audience in mind, they produce work that matters. The message becomes important. Ms. Garcia explains this feeling when she said in a group interview, "I think the writing is real-world. They get to see that there's a purpose for what they're doing. It's not to pass a test."

## 7. Revision matters.

Across the projects, revision was a not a step that followed drafting or composing, as is the case with a more traditional and linear writing process. Instead, revision was ongoing and integral to the process and was afforded by many opportunities to write, to collaborate, and to use technological tools to aid students in "re-visioning" their work.

Often, the nature and design of the projects made revision purposeful to the process and product, because writing activities were used as tools for structuring—and re-structuring—thinking (Ong 2002). In the elementary moviemaking project, students first wrote stories individually, but then students revised their stories multiple times as a result of various writing activities, including conferring with university preservice teachers, preparing a pitch, incorporating ideas from their peers to create a group story, storyboarding, and presenting their stories in script form.

Technological tools also allowed a natural and fluid revision process. For middle school students creating visual nonfiction essays, students composed and revised simultaneously; they continually made adjustments to their presentations because they could create new content and then immediately review and debate all aspects of that content—the visual appeal, the voiceover narration, the mood of the music, and so forth—and modify and augment this content before moving on to create more content. For both the elementary and middle school students finalizing their videos, they could play back scenes, discuss what was working well and what was not, and then make adjustments.

Revision, then, was enmeshed in both projects as critical and purposeful, and students developed an expanded view of the writing process and came away with understanding that time spent revising was time well spent.

## 8. Genre learning matters.

As members of the digital age, students readily consume hours and hours of messages presented in visual form. But what is remarkable about this fact is that they have had few school experiences that allow them to think about how media are made (Buckingham 2003; Messaris 1994; Prensky 2001). Across the projects, students engaged in genre forms that were fairly or entirely new to them. Interestingly, students' learning about new genres often brought about revelations about themselves as writers.

The elementary students, budding screenwriters, developed a new appreciation for the level of attention that screenwriters pay to every aspect of a script. These students quickly realized that writing a script was not a matter of taking their prose stories and chopping them up to put into a script format. Leslie blogged, *Today we're doing scriptwriting and at first it was easy but then it got hard. Now I understand that the more details you put in the story the better it is!* Leslie's comment stemmed from the fact that the students learned that a script is an essential roadmap for the actors, directors, costume and set designers—everyone involved in the filming. Classmate Alissa seconded Leslie's impression when she blogged, *It takes a lot of time to think about details we want in the script.* Another student, Jessica, learned to think about how all the parts contribute to a whole; she shared, *Sometimes you cut or add a scene to make it better.* This is a writing principle that she can apply to all her writing in the future.

Writing in a new genre form opened up possibilities and added strategies to students' writing toolboxes. For one student, it even brought about renewal: Middle schooler Ramon wrote, *I used to love writing in elementary but then I stopped writing. This was a good experience.*

## 9. Teacher disposition matters.

One key to the success of each of the literacy projects was the teacher—not because the teachers directed each step of the process, but because they had developed the dispositions to allow students to take charge and co-construct their own learning (Jonassen, Peck, and Wilson 1999). In a group reflective interview, four teachers in the elementary project described this scenario:

> **Ms. Lachey:** These children are of the computer generation. Everything is moving. Everything they do is moving. It was just wonderful to watch. It was enjoyable to see them taking care of things on their own. They didn't come and ask you this or that.
>
> **Mr. Contreras:** They said, "I need to do this." And we said, "Okay. Go on."
>
> **Ms. Brown:** That's what teachers are supposed to be—the facilitators.
>
> **Ms. Garcia:** The students learned more from each other. They were empowered. They were in control of their own learning. This is what learning is supposed to be like. It's what school should look like.

Students "taking charge" is a powerful idea, but also a frightening one to many teachers. The teachers leading these projects understood that allowing students to guide their own learning required teachers to accept the fact that there would be bumps in the road. Middle school teacher Mrs. Newstead commented, "You have to let children make mistakes." She later added, "And sometimes they'll go in a direction that you don't think is right, but they're somehow able to make it turn out okay if you let them run the course."

Elementary teacher Ms. Lachey reflected:

> *I would come in every day and know that there would be lots of activity. The hallways were filled with children. They were in and out. But everything was getting done. They*

*would keep each other on track; they'd say, "you didn't do this, you didn't do that." There was so much going on, so much communication, so much connection.*

Because language arts teachers are literacy advocates first and foremost and often not experts in technology, they have to be open to using technology with their students that they themselves are not 100 percent sure of (Vannatta and Fordham 2004). The teachers across these projects structured the classrooms in such a way that allowed students to make choices, to engineer their own learning, and to set their own schedule, even if it meant that each student might be at a different place at a different time. The teachers believed that their students, if given the right guidance and support, would work through the process and in the end "surprise" the audience with a video that was beyond their expectations.

The teachers in these projects were risk takers, and that kind of disposition is important to model if the students themselves are to be risk takers.

## 10. Empowerment matters.

Empowerment relates to students' beliefs about learning and their ability to act on them. Cambourne (1989) suggested students will engage in learning when they believe they have the capability to do the learning, they believe the learning has a purpose in their lives, and they are able to live through the risks associated with conducting the learning. Both projects fulfilled these criteria because they positioned students as active, self-confident learners who should be allowed to take risks as they engaged in activities that extended what they knew about literacy as well as themselves as literacy learners.

The two literacy projects built on the students' strengths. The projects allowed the students to select the texts they read, the topics they wrote about, the revisions they made, and the learning they pursued. With all of these choices, the students found spaces where they could excel. In the elementary project, students had the opportunity to apply for moviemaking jobs, such as actors, camera operators, and directors. In Carlos's application for director, he wrote, with a little humor, *I am good at telling people what to do, and I have a loud voice so everyone can hear me.* In the middle school project, Emelia wrote, *I learned more about working in groups and sharing the load of this project.* In many instances along the way, students reflected on the talents and skills they brought to the project. They took stock of who they are as people and as learners and as coworkers alongside their peers.

The design of the projects afforded the students the opportunity to become the architects of their learning (Goodman 2003). This opportunity motivated, challenged, and ultimately empowered the students; what follows is a small sampling of students' comments on what they gained from participating in the technology-infused writing projects.

## Elementary Students

At various points throughout the project, students shared their insights on their class blog. For example, Laila learned to think about audience:

> It's hard to write a whole story and then a script but we just have to keep thinking of stuff that will excite our viewers and readers.

Dora learned the value of many ideas:

> Some college students [university preservice teachers] came to my class to help me revise my rough draft! After that I had more ideas!! The morning was great because ideas were flying by with the [university] students. I bet my story is way better now!

Julian learned about story structure:

> Today we have finished the narrative and now we are doing a storyboard. We are drawing a picture and we are writing the most important parts of the movie we are going to do. We start at the rising action then we go to the climax then we go to the falling action, that's the last part.

Leslie learned about scriptwriting:

> Today we're doing scriptwriting and at first it was easy but then it got hard. Now I understand that the more details you put in the story the better [the script] is!

Rachel learned about the intricacies of moviemaking:

> If I want to make a movie I know I'm going to work hard, harder than I thought it would be because I thought all it would take was the script, camera, setting, and the actors but it doesn't just take that. It takes a lot of stuff to make a movie.

## Middle School Students

The middle school students reflected on what they gained as learners from participating in the project:

> I learned that the topic you choose can make the biggest difference on your project's outcome. You have to make sure it's not too narrow or too broad in order to get enough information. (Emelia)

*I learned how to be better organized in my research. (Keith)*

*I learned that you can't always find what you are looking for and it's good to improvise. (Arial)*

*I learned how to become a better video maker. (Teresa)*

*I learned how to work with new software. (Jessica)*

*I learned that it takes a lot of time and patience. But you need that if [the project] is going to be good. (Melissa)*

*I learned more about how to organize my ideas and gained more experience doing a voice-over. (Sergio)*

■ ■ ■ ■ ■

We think these ten reasons are what literacy teachers want to see in their classrooms. Now that you have a taste of these two projects and students' responses to them, we hope you'll want to know more about the nuts and bolts. Read on, and as you do, notice that in the margins we have identified some of the exemplary moments in which the classroom practices made writing with technology matter. In your own classrooms, you and your students are likely to discover even more reasons.

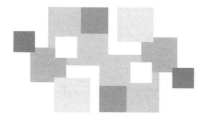

# Part 1
# Reading and Writing to Launch Moviemaking

As the lights dimmed, the audience quieted and the humming projector cast a long beam of light to the large screen on the stage at the front of the school auditorium. The 135 fourth- and fifth-grade students—along with family members, friends, and school personnel—knew the big moment of premiering their movies had arrived. This exciting day was the finale of a language arts and technology project that integrated reading, writing, and moviemaking.

It was not surprising that these students were excited. They were excited from day one when they learned that they would be making movies. But instead of putting cameras in students' hands immediately, the project's content was designed to engage students in reading and writing in order to support their moviemaking efforts.

The teachers were excited too, but not simply because their students had poured their hearts into the movies they created. The teachers were excited because of the learning that the integrated technology and language arts curriculum inspired.

So what exactly happened in these classrooms? In this section, you'll get an overview of the reading, writing, and moviemaking process, the technology students used (see Figures 1 and 2), and the how, the why, and the potential for making writing with technology matter to students.

Figure 1 *Process Overview*

**Researching Books to Read**
Reading and Blogging About Books

**Writing the Stories**
Pitching the Stories
Revising the Selected Stories
Conferring
Creating Storyboards
Adapting Stories to Scripts

**Learning About the Jobs of Moviemakers**
Filming the Movies
Editing with Microsoft Windows Movie Maker

Figure 2 *Technology Overview*

Blogging
Conducting a WebQuest
Analyzing media messages
Using scriptwriting software
Applying for a job online
Operating a video camera
Editing with Microsoft Windows Movie Maker

# Chapter 2
# Reading: Using Literature to Spark Ideas

If students are making movies, why start with reading books? Before the cameras roll, you must have something to film—a story. And to get students thinking about story, they must read. You have to put books in their hands. Reading literature gets students thinking about genre, structure, story elements . . . all of the things that make a good story. And well-chosen books have the potential to offer students material to draw from, a starting place for creating their own stories that can be made into movies.

## Researching Books to Read

Selecting books that will inspire students to create their own story lines is an important decision.

Although it is common today for students to have free rein to self-select books to read in literacy classrooms, in a project like this one, it may be wise to do some preselecting. Offering four to six books to the class will give your students enough choices to find a book that piques their interests. (See Figure 2.1 and Figure 2.2.) Choose books that have intriguing characters, fast-paced plots and a good amount of action, and endings that make readers wonder what could happen next.

Figure 2.1 [part 1] *Book Titles and Summaries for Elementary Grades*

Benton, J. 2004. *Dear Dumb Diary: My Pants Are Haunted*. New York: Scholastic.

Jaime Kelly, a self-described fashion expert and makeover guru, blames her beagle, Stinker, for ruining pair after pair of jeans—but it's really her mother's washing that is ruining them. When her mother buys her a pair of Bellazure jeans out of guilt, things start to go wrong. Jaime and her best friend, Isabella, believe that these haunted pants are to blame for causing them to slip down on the popularity chain at their middle school. Fortunately, a popular girl, Angelina, wants to buy the pants from Jaime, and Jaime agrees—but not before Stinker has a chance to rip up the knees as revenge for being blamed for ruining Jaime's other pants. When Angelina wears them at school, the other kids think it's a new trend. Because Angelina credits Jaime and Isabella for the ripped look of the jeans, the two girls' popularity increases just a bit.

Figure 2.1 [part 2] *Book Titles and Summaries for Elementary Grades*

Boniface, W. 2006. *The Extraordinary Adventures of Ordinary Boy: The Hero Revealed*. New York: HarperCollins.

Superopolis, a city where everyone except Ordinary Boy has superpowers, is home to a host of superheroes and Professor Brain-Drain, a very successful criminal mastermind. Life is full of adventure and intrigue as Ordinary Boy and his friends set out to solve the mystery surrounding their hero, the Amazing Indestructo, while trying to overcome the evil of Professor Brain-Drain. Along the way, Ordinary Boy learns that he is not so ordinary after all!

Collins, S. 2003. *Gregor the Overlander*. New York: Scholastic.

Eleven-year-old Gregor and his two-year-old sister, Boots, fall through a grate in their apartment's laundry room. They then find themselves in a mysterious underground world in which humans, rats, roaches, and bats coexist but not peacefully. Vikus, the leader of the Underlanders, believes that Gregor is the warrior in an ancient prophesy that foretells the Underland's future. Gregor goes on a quest that may save the Underlanders from the vicious rats as well as lead him to his father, who himself fell through the grate and is believed to be in imminent danger. The ensuing battle reveals whether Gregor, his sister, and his father return home safely.

Coville, B. 1989. *My Teacher Is an Alien*. New York: Aladdin.

Susan Simmons is surprised when her regular sixth-grade teacher, Ms. Schwartz, mysteriously doesn't return from spring vacation, and her class is stuck with a substitute, Mr. Smith. Susan's disappointment turns to horror when she discovers that Mr. Smith is actually an alien with a secret plot to recruit five students from Susan's class for an "educational mission" aboard a spaceship. Because she fears no adult will believe her, Susan enlists her bookworm friend and the class "creep" to help thwart Mr. Smith's plan and save Ms. Schwartz in the process.

Spinelli, J. 1992. *Report to the Principal's Office*. New York: Scholastic.

It's the first day of middle school, and four sixth graders are experiencing the jitters. Sunny Wyler is disgruntled about having to go to a new school without her best friend, Hillary. Sunny decides to do whatever it takes to get kicked out of her school so that she can be with Hillary. Meanwhile, Eddie Mott has a horrible first day and refuses to leave the bus. Salem Brownmiller, an aspiring writer, latches on to Eddie, thinking he is the perfect source for her dramatic stories. Pickles must report to the principal's office for having a skateboard. These four sixth graders are invited by the principal to lunch with him. The result is that unlikely friendships begin to develop, and soon, Sunny begins to rethink her plan for leaving.

Figure 2.1 [part 3] *Book Titles and Summaries for Elementary Grades*

West, T., and K. Noll. 2008. *Aly and AJ's Rock-n-Roll Mysteries: First Stop, New York*. New York: Penguin.

It is a rollicking time in New York City when Aly and AJ, two young, hip rock stars, come to the big city to perform in a rock concert and appear at the opening of the Girls Rock Academy. But smiles turn to frowns when they discover that guitars from the Girls Rock Academy have gone missing. They decide to help solve the mystery and in the process encounter many unexpected twists and turns. In the end, all is well, and Aly and AJ invite all their new friends to rock-and-roll with them at their concert.

Figure 2.2 [part 1] *Book Titles and Summaries for Middle School Grades*

Abbott, T. 2007. *Firegirl*. New York: Little, Brown.

Jessica Feeney, a badly burned seventh grader, attends a new school while she receives treatments at a local hospital. Afraid of her, her classmates shy away from her except for Tom, an overweight boy. As their relationship develops, both learn about the power of acceptance and friendship.

Collins, S. 2010. *The Hunger Games*. New York: Scholastic.

The story is set in Panem, the post-North American ruins that are now divided into twelve districts and ruled with harsh control. Sixteen-year-old Katniss Everdeen is chosen, along with a boy whom Katniss likes, Peeta, to represent their district in the annual Hunger Games, a fight-to-the-death battle among teens presented on live TV in which only one winner exists—the last one standing. But Katniss and Peeta unite to survive and add elements of love and humanity to the brutal game. Readers will begin to question how governments control their citizens and punish those who do not conform.

Preus, M. 2011. *Heart of a Samurai*. New York: Abrams.

Four Japanese teenage fishermen are rescued by an American whaleboat captain after they are caught in a storm. The year is 1841, and the Americans are viewed as barbarians and the Japanese as cannibals. But one teenager, Manjiro, braves the fears of the unknown and accepts the offer by the American captain to return with him to America. There he experiences racism, but rises above it to become much more than the fisherman he was destined to be.

Figure 2.2 [part 2] *Book Titles and Summaries for Middle School Grades*

Riordan, R. 2009. *The Lightning Thief.* New York: Hyperion.

Percy Jackson has upset the mythological monsters and the gods of Mount Olympus who have seemed to walk out of the pages of his mythological textbook at boarding school and into his life. Percy is believed to have stolen Zeus's lightning bolt, so Percy and his friends have but a few days to find and return the missing lightning bolt and thus restore peace to Mount Olympus.

Ryan, P. M. 2002. *Esperanza Rising.* New York: Scholastic.

Set in the 1930s, the life of a wealthy Mexican girl changes when her father is murdered and her family is forced to flee to the United States where they work as migrant workers to survive. As Esperanza grows into her new situation, she sends out a message of hope and perseverance for all people.

Soto, G. 2003. *Taking Sides.* Boston, MA: Houghton Mifflin Harcourt.

Eighth grader Lincoln Mendoza moves from a Hispanic barrio to a wealthy white suburb. Trying to adjust to his new situation, he feels tension when he faces his old friends in a basketball game. As the game day approaches, Lincoln wonders which team he wants to win. He must decide how to deal with his loyalties divided between the life he left behind and the new one he is living.

Woodson, J. 2010. *After Tupac and D Foster.* New York: Penguin.

Two best friends are growing up together in a close-knit African American neighborhood, identifying with Tupac Shakur's lyrics and dreaming about their "big purpose" in life. Then one day D Foster enters into the mix and opens up their world. Living in a foster home, D Foster has freedom to go and come as she pleases, but secretly she longs for her real mama and has a secret to protect. Woodson weaves in subplots that address homosexuality, fatherlessness, jail visits, and foster children as she captures the girls' passage from childhood to adolescence.

Other factors to consider when selecting texts could be genre, theme, protagonist(s), length, and adaptability of text:

- *Genre.* Offer books from at least a couple of genres. Fantasy lends itself to creative and imaginative thinking; in terms of making movies, students who choose to read and write in the fantasy genre could incorporate special effects and unique characters in their stories. Realistic fiction is familiar and relatable to students; from the practical perspective of making movies, the settings usually take place in available locales (such as schools and homes), and many of the characters can be portrayed by their peers because they are similar in age. Historical fiction provides opportunities for students to conduct research; when making movies, students can incorporate artifacts in the props and backdrops in order to re-create the time period authentically.
- *Theme.* Select books that present prominent themes students can easily relate to and work with when writing their own stories, such as dealing with loss, overcoming challenges, teamwork, and being true to oneself.
- *Protagonist(s).* Choose books with a male or female protagonist who is similar in age or slightly older than the students. The most appealing books will feature protagonists who are dealing with issues that the students themselves likely face.
- *Length.* The books selected in this moviemaking project ranged from about 120 pages to just over 300 pages. Interestingly, length did not factor significantly in students' selection of books. Relatability to characters and action-filled plot lines were the major attractions, so students were willing to go the distance with longer texts. However, from a practical perspective, all students will need to finish reading their books about the same time, so some may have to do some reading outside of class to stay at the same pace.
- *Adaptability of text.* The texts selected will need to lend themselves to being adapted in some way. For instance, open-ended books can be extended as sequels, while a fascinating main character begs for a prequel. For other books, settings or points of view can be changed.

In order for students to have enough information to make a well-informed book choice, they can conduct a WebQuest, an inquiry-oriented activity in which students gain information about the books from web sources. Teachers do the initial planning for a WebQuest by locating online sources that provide information about the preselected texts. These sources can include official author websites, book review sites, and bookseller sites such as Barnes and Noble and Amazon. Teachers can review the content within these sites to check for age-level appropriateness; they might also need to ensure that the sites are approved—not blocked or censored—by the school district. Teachers should then compile a

Research

list of the links that they will provide students. (See Appendix A: "Handout: Conducting a WebQuest" to use while guiding your students as they complete the WebQuest.)

Students can share their research findings from their WebQuest and then choose either the text they researched or a text they heard about from their peers.

# Reading and Blogging About Books

As students read their books, they need opportunities to share their thoughts and feelings as well as their puzzlements. Literature circle groups, ideally about four or five members each and formed based on common book selections, are a great way to accomplish this.

In anticipation of moviemaking, keep in mind that the number of books students select determines the minimum number of movies that they will eventually produce. In other words, if it is feasible to make two movies in your classroom, then form literature circles around two texts.

**Engagement**

Traditionally students in literacy classrooms have participated in literature circle chats with their peers and responded in journals read by their teachers. Technology, via a class blog, can add to the experience.

- Students have a wider audience. Two literature groups reading the same text can share and compare their thinking. And all students, regardless of their text selection, can read the blog to see what's happening in other literature circles.
- Students are afforded more "think time" than is possible in face-to-face discussions.
- Students' thinking is made public, which tends to cause the bloggers to be purposeful and thoughtful about their ideas and opinions before (and while) putting them in writing. Also, postings become a living document that students can return to later to reread their thoughts and their peers' thoughts.
- All students have a chance to share; no "talk hogs" allowed, and no one is silenced, not even introverted students.
- Students are not restricted by classroom schedules since bloggers need not respond at a particular pace or time of day.

Given this kind of space, students can take their responses in a number of directions. When students in this moviemaking project responded to their reading in personal journals, their writing tended to consist of recording major plot events. However, students responding on the blog tended not to summarize; rather, their posts generally were continuations of the rich talk that was part of the literature circles. Consequently, students began shifting toward sharing deeper connections and showing higher-level thinking. For example, Marie, deeply invested in the lives of the characters in her book, had an emotional reaction when one of the characters died:

*Gregor the Overlander is kind of sad, but it's cool. I wonder why a good character had to die!!! (I cried a lot when a good "thing" died) You should read it. Get your tissues ready!!!*

Sometimes, students' responses were influenced by ideas and connections beyond the plots of the books. Caleb, drawing on his own literacy history, indicated that he knew Andrew Clements wrote both *Lunch Money* (2005) and *Frindle* (1996):

*I read Lunch Money and I think it is even better than Frindle! The story is solid, like all of his books. The thing that separates it from his other books is the way the characters are. My rating is Story: 10/10 Characters: 10/10 Art: 8/10 Drama: 6/10 Overall: 9/10.*

In this post, Caleb showed evaluative thinking by making a judgment—*Lunch Money* is better than *Frindle*. He also appropriated the features of movie reviews by rating some story elements on a ten-point scale. In his opinion, the elements that spoke to the quality of a work were story, characters, art, drama, and an overall experience. Students who came across Caleb's post saw a new way of thinking and responding to books that they might incorporate in their own blog postings.

For teacher tips on blogging, see Figure 2.3.

**Figure 2.3** *Teacher Tips on Blogging*

There are really only about three instructional approaches for steering a blogging community:

- The "Training Wheels" approach: The teacher introduces the purpose and process for blogging and initially assigns guiding, open-ended questions to focus students' responses.
- The "Copilot" approach: Instead of using a direct instruction model, the teacher participates as a blogger with the students, modeling appropriate response patterns.
- The "Hands Off" approach: Without much introduction and limited guidance, students participate as posters on a blog, essentially learning appropriate response patterns from one another along the way.

Once students have read engaging texts that have given them lots of ideas to think about, they are ready to create their own stories. In the next chapter, we explore how teachers can guide students through a dynamic and authentic writing process.

# Chapter 3
# Writing: Transforming Ideas into Stories

Movies are made from scripts, and scripts are written stories. So for students to progress toward making movies, they have to write stories that can be turned into scripts. The question is, how to begin?

## Writing the Stories

Fortunately, many students gain plenty of story ideas from reading their book selections. The students are essentially partnering with a book's author who has thought deeply about the story—the characters, the plot, the setting, the conflict and resolution, the theme, and so forth. *Collaboration* is so much easier than facing a blank page; the task, then, is deciding how to home in on one idea.

Enter the "Poster of Possibilities," a list of ideas for adapting or extending texts, and the "Poster of Genres," a list of genres for students to consider for their movies. (See Figures 3.1 and 3.2; see also Appendix A: "Mini-Lesson: Poster of Possibilities.") Encourage students to ponder the strengths of the original books and use the two posters to brainstorm some changes they could make in their own stories. For example, a popular choice might be to extend the events of the book by writing a sequel; in terms of genres, a popular choice might be to transform events from a realistic fiction book into fantasy or vice versa. (See Figure 3.3.)

After they narrow down their ideas, students should then create a first draft of their stories. Students will be able to draw from the well-developed texts they read and discussed in literature circles and reflected on in journals and on the class blog. The draft should be rich enough so that the story feels complete, but does not need to go through the traditional

Figure 3.1 *Poster of Possibilities*

Move your characters to another setting.

Rewrite the story as if it happened in your world, with your friends and family.

Tell the story from a different character's point of view.

Write the story with a visitor from another novel.

Plan another outcome.

Write the sequel.

Write the prequel.

Change a character's personality.

**POSTER OF POSSIBILITIES**
**The only limit is your imagination!**

Figure 3.2 *Poster of Genres*

*Contemporary Realistic Fiction*
- Plot events could actually happen.
- Stories take place in modern times.

*Modern Fantasy*
- Some elements are not realistic, such as magic or talking animals.
- Stories are imaginative and often set in other worlds with unique societies.

*Science Fiction*
- Plots involve science and technology of the future.
- Story lines might explore important issues in society or make predictions about life in the future.

*Historical Fiction*
- Plot events are based around a historical time period or event.
- Dialogue is invented for characters that are based on real people.

*Mystery*
- Main character is trying to solve a puzzling situation or event.
- Plots intentionally keep readers guessing.

Figure 3.3 *Examples of Adaptations from* My Teacher Is an Alien

| Introduced new characters. | "To make the movie funnier, we added three kids: one of them eats glue, one of them reacts to the movies, and one of them has blue ears." |
| | "We added a character. The teacher now has a daughter. The teacher faints at the beginning of the story. If nobody had been there, the teacher would have just been lying there. We needed someone to help the teacher." |
| Deleted characters. | "We took Duncan away. He was the school bully in the book. We didn't really need him. He didn't have a big part. Since we needed to make the movie short, we took him away." |
| Changed the mood. | "In our movie, we didn't want anything bad or sad. We just wanted it to be entertainment." |
| Changed the roles of the characters, affecting the plotline. | "We changed it from the teacher being the alien to all the students are the aliens." |

stages of the writing process, such as revision, editing, and publishing. Again, it is enough simply to get ideas in motion.

# Pitching the Stories

*Pitching* is a process professional screenwriters endure in everyday life—having to sell their ideas to agents or studio executives. Students learning about pitching and writing and delivering their own pitch is an important step for a number of reasons:

Process

- It's how Hollywood does it, so it's an authentic step in the moviemaking process.
- It's an art form and therefore exposes students to a new genre.
- It involves critical thinking about messages and requires application of several important reading skills, such as summarizing and synthesizing, word choice, and awareness of audience.
- It allows students to practice and sharpen speaking and listening skills.

Teachers will need to build students' knowledge about the art form of pitching because they might think that pitching involves simply standing in front of the classroom and reading their stories from beginning to end. Consequently, teachers should introduce the components of a good pitch:

Genre
Learning

- It starts with a teaser or hook to grab the attention of the audience.
- It identifies the genre and summarizes the story idea briefly by focusing on the main characters and conflict—without giving too much away.
- It's delivered with high energy and excitement.

After this brief introduction, students can learn more about pitching by analyzing messages in familiar forms of media, such as movie trailers and previews. Invite your students to think about how media producers entice their audiences through the use of color, music, sound effects, and so forth. (See Appendix A: "Mini-Lesson: The Pitch.")

In "The Pitch" mini-lesson, we emphasize that writing a pitch requires careful thinking. Students have to bring a number of reading, writing, and speaking skills to the table. Summarizing, in the case of constructing a pitch, forces students to home in on critical aspects of text. Because a pitch is spoken, word choice is critical; specifically, students have to think about choosing just the right word to produce a desired effect, whether it's shock, surprise, or suspense, for instance. Students also have to make decisions about how to reveal the genre of their stories. And, of course, they have to decide how to deliver their pitch to increase the effectiveness and impact of their words on the audience.

Audience

After students create their pitches, they need ample time to practice their pitch delivery—multiple times, even; after all, they have just one shot to sell their ideas to their peers. Teachers might want to capitalize on this authentic speaking experience by helping students understand effective techniques related to intonation, pacing, expression, and so forth.

Pitching in this project also serves a more practical—and critical—purpose: narrowing the number of movies that can be produced. Teachers have to make a decision about the number of movies that can be realistically produced; the decision may be influenced either by the available resources or by the number of groups the teacher feels he or she can adequately manage. Let's do some simple math. There are twenty-five students in the classroom. These students are divided among five literature circle groups. Is there enough time and resources for each group to produce one movie for a total of five movies? If so, then that's easy: Every member of a particular literature circle pitches their story and one of those is selected for production. Or, you can avoid doing math altogether and just pick one pitch for each text.

Selecting the stories from the pitches that will move forward can be done either through classroom voting—by a show of hands or privately by casting ballots—or by inviting a group of impartial judges to vote, such as school personnel or students from another class and/or grade level. No matter how the winning pitches are determined, it will be important for teachers to reinforce the idea that pitching is one step in a multistep process and that all students will be important contributors in the next steps whether or not their story pitches are selected to be made into movies.

## Revising the Selected Stories

Collaborative writing is another process professional writers engage in. Just as the stories behind movies are often constructed collaboratively, the students with the winning pitches can benefit from working with students in the class who read the same text and have their own ideas to contribute. Working in small groups, collaborators should begin the hard work of transforming a first-draft story into a polished, shared vision for a story worthy of appearing on screen. When a group sits down to work together, they should have these sources to draw from:

*Collaboration*

- The pitch that won.
- The story that backed the pitch that won.
- The other group members' individual stories and pitches.
- The text itself from which all the group members' stories were based.

*Revision*

The students who participated in this moviemaking project offered and considered many ideas, often from their individual stories, in order to determine the ones that would best enhance the group story; most times, students realized that even a small detail was a welcome addition and strengthened a particular story element. Following are examples of how group members' input influenced the text based on *Gregor the Overlander* (Collins 2003).

| INDIVIDUAL STORY | GROUP STORY |
|---|---|
| Gregor is in his apartment. He finds an open grate with wisps of vapor. | Gregor is in the laundry room doing the laundry. "Where's the soap?" he says. He sees a bit of mist coming from outside a door. "What is that? Holy smokes, I'm falling!! HHHEEELLPPP!" Gregor starts falling down a tunnel. |

In the group's version, the setting is more precise—Gregor is in the laundry room, not the apartment. The addition of critical details (*doing the laundry*; *he sees a bit of mist*) slows down the action and paints a picture of what the main character is doing. Students also added dialogue to show the character's confusion and feelings:

| INDIVIDUAL STORY | GROUP STORY |
|---|---|
| They walked a short way to a prison and Gregor finally sees his father's face after two years. | Nerissa says, "I will lead you to the prison where your father is." Ripred says, "Follow me." They head to Gregor's father's hideout. Nerissa says, "Go in, go in." Gregor walks to see his father. |

Clarifying the generic *they* in the original story, the group divided the action between the characters Nerissa and Ripred and added appropriate dialogue. To increase the tension and add suspense, the group added Nerissa's urging, "Go in, go in."

| INDIVIDUAL STORY | GROUP STORY |
|---|---|
| "AAAHHH!" screamed Gregor. "I'm going to KILL whoever did this!!!" He turned purplish white and his eyes turned pitch black. Midnight purple. Electricity streamed its way out of him. A horrible transformation turned him into a monster. | "AAAHHH!" screamed Gregor. Gregor's dad had passed away, and Gregor was so enraged that he turned into something horrible: the feared Eco monster!!! |

Sensory language was lost in the revision above. Although the individual story "showed" the transformation, the group's shortened version only "told" about the transformation.

Taken as a whole, the strength of collaboration is that multiple voices with multiple perspectives rise and join together to influence a text. Sometimes there is great variety and depth to the revisions, such as a group's decision to slow down the scene to increase tension and suspense, and sometimes great parts may be lost while the text is still transforming into a greater whole. Such is the revision process.

# Conferring

Process

Consider creating opportunities for students to receive additional input about their writing. By reaching out to peers from other classrooms, campuses, or adults such as parents, campus personnel, or university students, students can gain new, outside perspectives. These conferences can be face-to-face or conducted online through blogging or messaging. (See Appendix A: "Handout: Tips for Conducting a Conference.")

Collaboration

The students participating in this moviemaking project met with university students studying to be teachers. As a result of being able to talk through their ideas and to hear an outsider's perspective, the students became more aware of the decisions required of authors to bridge the gap between what is in their heads and what is actually on the paper. In a group debrief following the conferences, students reported these observations about writing:

- "You need to really care about [the writing] so it will turn out good."
- "Writing takes a lot of detail to make the story interesting."
- "You need one specific idea so it is not just flipping all over the place."
- "You had to know where the beginning starts and how the problem resolved in the end."
- "You should try to move the audience."
- "When you write, you have to catch the person as soon as you can so they will stick to reading it."
- "I want the audience to be anxious to see what is next. I want the audience to say, 'Wow. That is a good idea. [The writers] must be really creative.'"

Audience

Another benefit of students having the opportunity to discuss their ideas with someone other than a peer is that they were reminded that what they were creating would be viewed by a larger audience—which also is reflected in some of their comments.

# Creating Storyboards

In a traditional literacy classroom, with a polished story in hand, students would find themselves at the end of a process. This integrated technology and language arts project, however, keeps students in a dynamic, recursive state of thinking about texts, talking about texts, writing about texts, and revising and refining their ideas.

One tool students can use to refine and reflect on their ideas is a storyboard. A storyboard is a sequence of boxes containing pictures and text to help visualize a story as a whole (Essley, Rief, and Rocci 2008). Because of students' familiarity with comic strips and graphic novels, storyboarding is a tool that students will likely gravitate to. Interestingly, storyboarding looks deceptively simple—it seems as though a writer merely places the main events of a story chronologically from start to end. However, along the way, the writer is forced to make many decisions, such as what events should or should not be included, what level of detail is needed to convey those events and ideas, what gaps exist in the story line and how they should be addressed, and so forth. Truly, storyboarding causes students to think about their ideas in a new way yet again in this process.

*Process*

In this project, the tool can be used to help students figure out how to break up their prose into scenes. This is an important step in helping students really understand that they are shifting their thinking from putting words on a page to putting images on a screen. To introduce students to storyboarding, see Appendix A for a mini-lesson called "Storyboarding." The mini-lesson helps students understand the thinking behind a storyboard and then asks them to create one for their group's story using paper and drawing supplies.

You may be wondering why, in a book about technology in the literacy classroom, we suggest completing a storyboard with paper and pencil. Creating storyboards in Microsoft Office PowerPoint is possible because of the ability to move slides around, use stock photos and images, and type text. However, there are several limitations:

*Revision*

1. The electronic storyboarding process can be more time-consuming than paper-based storyboarding.
2. Students have to try to find images that match what is in their minds.
3. Students can see only one slide at a time, thus making attention to sequencing more difficult.

Most important, PowerPoint lends itself to creating polished presentations, and thus blurs the purpose of creating a storyboard. Storyboarding is not about creating a product, but about using a tool to organize thinking. Therefore, traditional pen and paper may trump technology in this instance.

In Figure 3.4, a storyboard that students created based on the book *Gregor the Overlander* included plot events, special effects, camera positions, and dialogue. Additionally, students ensured that each frame was richly detailed; elements included:

- Purposeful illustrations that reflected the action and special effects that they envisioned in their heads (see "Zoom!" in Frame 1 and the lightning in Frame 5).
- Characters that were labeled (see Frames 2, 3, 7 and 8).
- Color that was used to emphasize important ideas (see Frame 4: "Gregor's dad is no longer with us").
- Eraser marks and scratching out of text that showed how they discussed their ideas and changed their minds (see Frames 1, 2, 4, 7, and 8).
- Added words that indicated how students fine-tuned their ideas. For example, in Frame 5, initially only the word *monster* appeared. After some discussion, another student added the words *Gregor turns into a* before the word *monster*. Similarly, in Frame 6, students wrote the title *Army of RATS* and another student added the word *coming*.

Figure 3.4 *A Storyboard Based on the Book* Gregor the Overlander *(Collins 2003)*

# Adapting Stories to Scripts

Professional writers know that creating a script involves more than simply typing up a story in a different form. To help your students learn to adapt the genre of fiction to the genre of drama, teach mini-lessons about how books compare to movies. (See Appendix A: "Mini-Lesson: Comparing a Book to a Movie" and "Mini-Lesson: Tools for Authors and Scriptwriters/Moviemakers.")

*Genre Learning*

Transforming stories into scripts ushers in another opportunity for revision using technological tools. Huddled around computers and aided by the scriptwriting software of your choice (usually downloadable for free, such as from www.scripped.com), students can make line-by-line decisions about how best to transition their ideas from print form to the screen.

*Revision*

Students will quickly discover that scriptwriting is a structure that forces writers to "re-vision" their work. Expect stories to swell in size as they transform from ones to be read to scripts to be enacted. For example, a "telling" sentence in a story will not work well for the screen; therefore, students have to write a great deal of new content in which characters interact, express feelings, reveal motivations, and so forth.

One group wrote their story, based on *Lunch Money* (Clements 2005), and then re-wrote it for the screen:

| STORY |
|---|
| Anthony is bummed that he has to go to this school, however Zeke likes it. Anthony also mentions that cooking class may be the only good class. |

| SCRIPT | |
|---|---|
| **Anthony:** | Man, another year of disappointment. I can't believe it. |
| **Zeke:** | Come on, get psyched! This is the best year of my life! There's got to be a class you like! |
| **Anthony:** | Well, at least cooking might be fun. |

In the story, the writers *tell* readers how Anthony and Zeke feel. Anthony is bummed about the school and Zeke likes it. In the script, the addition of rich dialogue *shows* Anthony's feeling of being bummed (*Man, another year of disappointment.*) and Zeke's excitement (*Come on, get psyched! This is the best year of my life!*). Writing a script forces students to show, not tell.

Genre
Learning

From studying scripts, students will recognize that a script has many jobs to do because it is the blueprint for making a film: It tells the actors how to perform their roles, both verbally and nonverbally; it provides directors with a document from which he or she then makes important decisions, including a filming schedule; it is used by set designers to prepare essential props and backdrops before shooting; and it offers directions to camera operators.

It may be helpful to use a model to show students the kinds of changes they will need to make as they transform their stories into scripts. (See Appendix A: "Mini-Lesson: Turning a Story into a Script.")

■ ■ ■ ■ ■ ■ ■

With scripts in hands, the moviemaking process can now begin. In the next chapter, we provide information on teaching students how moviemakers transform words from a script to images on the big screen.

# Chapter 4
# Moviemaking: Turning Stories into Movies

Lights! Camera! Action! Students will likely view the moviemaking process as the fun part, not realizing that it is a complex activity that requires skill and craft. In fact, although students are intent moviegoers and dedicated fans of popular movies, they are often unaware of what goes on behind the scenes and therefore have misconceptions about how movies are created. For example, Orlando, one student who participated in the project, thought "actors just make up the lines as they are acting," not realizing that they use scripts.

Moviemaking isn't easy or carefree or something that can be done in a day. It calls for orchestration—a cast and crew coming together to work in concert.

To launch the moviemaking phase of this project, teachers may want to distribute an evaluation rubric to students and discuss the categories upon which their work will be evaluated. (See Appendix A: "Handout: Moviemaking Rubric.") Teachers can then forecast for students the main components of moviemaking that we discuss in this chapter, from taking on moviemaking roles to filming the scenes to editing the movie to creating the final product.

## Learning About the Jobs of Moviemakers

Because the process of moviemaking will be a new experience for students as well as for many teachers, it is important to immerse students in the new genre beginning with learning about the various roles involved in making movies.

Get the moviemaking process off and running by putting a camera in the students' hands. Doing so raises the level of student engagement by showing them that they—not adults—will be responsible for creating the movies. However, because the experience will be new, teachers need to provide instruction with this technological tool, including safety tips, basic operations, and camera techniques, and give students the opportunity to put their new knowledge into practice. (See Appendix A: "Mini-Lesson: Operating a Camera.") Instruction is important for all students because it introduces terminology associated with the genre.

Once students have an understanding of one moviemaking job, they are ready to think about the jobs that happen in front of the camera, namely actors, as well as behind the scenes, such as set designers, directors, and camera operators. Using a popular book and movie adaptation, such as *Bridge to Terabithia* (Csupo 2007; Paterson 1977), which students may be familiar with from mini-lessons presented during the scriptwriting process (see Chapter 3), is a way to use a familiar source to help them find examples of the various tasks that each job requires. (See Appendix A: "Mini-Lesson: Moviemaking Jobs.")

**Empowerment**    Because the mini-lesson provides an overview of moviemaking roles, students will start thinking about how they can contribute to the moviemaking process and begin engaging in self-appraisal, taking stock of their natural talents, their previous experiences, and the skills that they want to develop. Rather than asking students to raise their hands to volunteer for specific jobs, teachers can take this opportunity to engage the students in a real-world writing task by having each one complete a mock job application. (See Appendix A: "Handout: Moviemaking Job Application.") Doing so empowers students because they are given a voice in a decision-making process, rather than being assigned a task by the teacher. Keeping with the idea of an authentic experience, consider posting the application on the class blog and having students reply electronically with their completed applications. Students should provide their qualifications for all of the roles because it might be necessary for them to perform more than one role.

The students who participated in this project applied for and accepted several jobs. Following are a few excerpts of the qualifications students listed on their job applications:

*For the position of actor:*
I really like to act. I can really cry real tears.

I'm good at talking out loud. I am not very nervous on camera. In school, I have performed in different things.

*For the position of camera operator:*
I have taken videos with a video camera. I almost know what every button on the camera is.

My sister had a lot of experience with cameras and she showed me how to use it.

*For the position of director:*
I am good at telling people what to do, and I have a loud voice so everyone can hear me.

I directed a skit and uploaded [the skit] on the Internet.

Clearly, some students thought that experience mattered most (*I directed a skit*), while others thought knowledge was important (*I almost know what every button on the camera is*). Still others emphasized perceived abilities and talents (*I am not very nervous on camera*). The reasons, although endearing, did not matter. What mattered was that students were assessing their own abilities and applying the talents they valued in themselves.

After students complete their job applications online, their roles will need to be determined. Depending on the number of films being made, it might be the case that students will need to assume multiple roles.

# Filming the Movies

As students assume the roles of actors, set designers, directors, and camera operators, teachers will likely need to help students further prepare for the main functions of each job:

- Actors need to learn about projecting their voices, expressing emotion, and taking cues from the script.
- Set designers may need help finding creative approaches for transforming everyday materials into props. (See Figure 4.1 for how one group of students made an outdoor scene out of paper.)
- Camera operators need help analyzing the scripts to make decisions about the kinds of shots and angles needed.
- Directors need to learn how to block scenes (determining the placement of the actors on the set), begin and end takes, and create a shot log (a record of the takes that the director approves and will turn over to producers/editors).

Essentially as the students start displaying their confidence and capabilities in their roles, the teacher's role changes from instructional leader to interested observer. In other words, once the teacher establishes a particular time line for filming (say, two or three days), it becomes incumbent upon the students to set the daily work schedule in order to meet the due date. Quickly the students will come to understand that their moviemaking roles are interdependent—for example, a director cannot have a camera operator film a scene until the set design is in place and the actors have memorized their lines. Collaboration becomes paramount as small tasks must come together to create the larger whole. Each individual's contribution comes to

Teacher
Disposition

Figure 4.1 *A Sample Set Design*

Critical
Thinking

light as students realize the importance of every task. This process mirrors the skills present in a workplace setting, such as taking responsibility, making and sticking to schedules, securing the necessary materials to complete a job, and even experiencing a little peer pressure. Gabriel, one of the students participating in the project, posted on the class blog that he was aware of his task list, was feeling the pressure of getting things done, and was wondering about the progress of other moviemakers:

> What I need to do is make an alien mask and a human mask. I also need to finish painting the airplane. We even need to stick the soldiers to the airplane. My group is almost finished; we just need to finish some settings. How about you?

With every student working in harmony to complete their tasks on time, filming should be easy, right? The reality, though, is that just as a good story goes through many drafts, a good movie requires multiple takes. An actor participating in this project reflected on the class blog about the need for multiple takes:

> Some of the scenes were easy but then others we had to practice a couple of times. Most of the scenes we had to get deeply in character. The scenes with a lot of expression were harder. I liked the scenes with action because you get to move rather than just talking to someone.

During the project, the actors were not the only ones who realized the need for multiple takes. A noisy hallway, an unexpected fire drill, or an uncontrollable fit of laughter can cause the director to yell, "Cut!" Directors yelled, "take two [or three or four . . .]!" after they huddled around the cameras, played back footage, and saw that the words on the script and the picture in their minds did not match the image in the camera. The result was that students were thrust into problem-solving mode—a desire to revise on the spot in order to narrow the gap between what they wanted their movie to look like and what the movie actually looked like. (See Figure 4.2.)

Figure 4.2 *Student Actors and Directors*

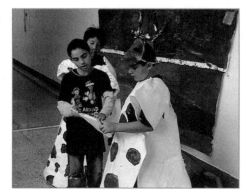

Similar to when they adapted their stories into scripts, students came to understand the need for depth and detail in order to communi-

Critical
Thinking

cate an idea. In the small viewing window of the camera, they needed to decide whether what they wrote translated well to what they saw and created on film. The camera is the catalyst for revision; when dissatisfied with what they see, students must work collaboratively and think critically about how to resolve the discrepancy.

The filming process, then, is not all fun and games. It's fun, yes, but it also requires teamwork, strategic planning, patience, endurance, and creative and flexible thinking in order to make decisions about the unexpected problems that confront or confound moviemakers. (See Figure 4.3.)

Figure 4.3 *Creative Moviemaking Solutions*

- How did students work around the fact that these movies weren't just *low* budget, they were *no* budget? With a little creativity, most everything could be made of paper, including a washer and dryer, a dog's costume, a bus, and mountains in Egypt.
- How did students tell viewers about important events that happened a year ago? Flashback, of course! Students even figured out that during filming, the characters had to wear different clothes and hairstyles to make the flashback authentic.
- How did students achieve flight? One group used a broomstick to lift a (paper) spaceship into the air. Another group placed a boy (carefully) atop a cart with wheels and manually pushed him through the scene. Then, presto, they had a flying superhero!

# Editing with Microsoft Windows Movie Maker

Once filming wraps, producing and editing begin—likely another new experience. Although students are the consumers of media in the digital age we live in, they may have had few opportunities to consider how media are produced. Erasmo, a student who participated in the project, illustrated this point when he posted on the class blog:

*What I didn't know about filming is that we were going to edit the movie.*

It is possible that many students may think that a moviemaker turns on a camera and films, from beginning to end, a movie—a final, finished product. The job of producing movies is multilayered but is made easier with a technological tool, Microsoft Windows Movie Maker software.

Microsoft Windows Movie Maker is typically available as a free download. Teachers can visit Microsoft's website for a short how-to tutorial to give students an overview of the editing process. After viewing the tutorial, teachers will want to take some time to discuss students' growing knowledge of the genre of filmmaking. For instance, students will have

Genre
Learning

learned that movies are shot in scenes, often multiple times; that the scenes are not necessarily filmed in sequential order; that film footage has to be edited and put together in a logical sequence; and that films are produced and enhanced with special effects, music, and so forth. Then students simply need the opportunity to experiment with the software's features, because, as is the case with many technological tools, the best way to learn them is to play with them. (See Figure 4.4.)

Figure 4.4 *Editors and Producers, Ready for Hollywood*

How did students make their movies memorable? Often with special effect techniques:

*Slow motion:* Slow motion was used by one group to dramatize a scene of one character tripping another in the school cafeteria. Another group used slow motion to create more tension during a fight scene between two foes.

*Music:* Music served many purposes, from creating the right mood at the beginnings or endings of movies to supporting the action in a particular scene. One group used ominous music for comedic effect in a scene where the main character thinks a pair of jeans has come alive to terrorize her.

*Voice-over narration:* Voice-over narration was used by one group to transition from one scene to another and enhanced by displaying the diary of the main character as the narrator read the entries to viewers.

*Authentic re-creation of settings:* One movie contained many scenes outside and inside a popular retail store. To increase the authenticity of their shots, students filmed the outside shots at the local mall and then re-created the interior of the store in a classroom. Another group wrote a scene in which the main characters held a news press conference; the editors added a ticker tape along the bottom of the screen in order to add authenticity.

*Bloopers:* Some groups included blooper reels because many shots, left on the cutting room floor, were too irresistible not to show viewers!

In order to begin constructing their movies, students will need a director's shot log. (See Figure 4.5.) The director's shot log provides producers/editors with the information they will need in order to know which clips and/or takes to use. Windows Movie Maker allows students to drag and drop these clips into a storyboard. Once students have sequenced their clips, students naturally move into an editing stage.

**Figure 4.5** *An Example of a Student Director's Shot Log*

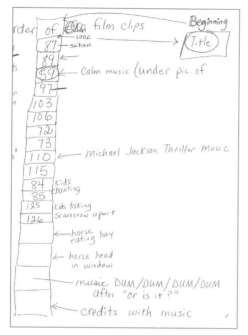

Using a technological tool during the editing stage makes for dynamic work because of the many options available. For example, students have to trim clips, select music, choose a background, add transitions, and use special effects such as aging and slow motion. Every decision leads to another decision because students are continually shaping the product. At any point during the editing and producing stages, students will be huddled around the computer screen as scenes are enhanced with voice-over narration or transitions; other students will have on headphones, searching for the perfect song to match a particular scene; still others will be considering fonts and backgrounds as they add titles and credits. Technological tools place students in a continual process of editing that they will see as relevant and necessary to producing a high-quality product. Jessica, one of the participating students, made this point:

*I've learned a bunch of stuff, like sometimes you cut or add a scene to make it better.*

Jessica articulated the purpose of editing—*to make it better*. Teachers have long yearned for students to want to revise, and here, Jessica saw the need for the task and took it on willingly. As educators, we can only hope that as Jessica successfully reflected on her recent moviemaking knowledge, she will remember the benefits of editing and apply her aha moment to her writing process in the future.

■ ■ ■ ■ ■

Taken as a whole, the experiences of reading, writing, and moviemaking will lead to an understanding of the process of putting ideas on film. Initial impressions that moviemaking is easy may transform into a deep admiration for those in the moviemaking industry; one student, Laila, made this point in one of her class blog posts in the final days of moviemaking:

*This process has been harder than I thought, actually. When I am looking at TV, I just [thought it's] so easy to make a movie or film. Now I am the one on camera. So I am right there with you, Hannah Montana.*

Teacher Disposition

Students who participate in a project like this one will be more knowledgeable producers—not unconscious consumers—of media. Teachers who guide a project like this one will be more knowledgeable about students' workplace and literacy skills. Furthermore, teachers will recognize that a multistep process allows for ongoing formative assessment and should be open to seeing their students' skills and talents in a different light than might be afforded with traditional literacy practices.

As the lights dimmed, the audience quieted and the humming projector cast a long beam of light onto the large screen on the stage at the front of the school auditorium. Students took on their final role, that of moviegoer.

# Part 2
# Authoring the Visual Nonfiction Essay

Bards and adventure, Crusades and loyalty, Vikings and deception, Rembrandt and romance, Leonardo da Vinci and riddles, Shakespeare and mystery. Middle school students researching the Medieval to the Post-Renaissance time periods explored these topics and themes and so many more.

The cross-curricular project in which students learned about the bubonic plague in science, the feudal system in history, and Renaissance paintings in art meant that students arrived in the English language arts classroom with extensive background knowledge of the eras.

With a sense of the big picture, the students were ready to begin the project-based study that led to authoring visual nonfiction essays. This research project involved students reading and discussing historical fiction, responding individually to their reading by composing texts in a variety of genres, conducting research, and producing visual nonfiction essays collaboratively.

But what is a visual nonfiction essay, anyway? Let's take the name and work backward. It's an essay, meaning it's a piece of student writing. It's nonfiction, meaning students conduct research to learn about a particular topic. It's visual, meaning students display their learning through the incorporation of images. Think of it as a twenty-first-century update of the traditional research paper in that students research both print texts and electronic sources, communicate with words as well as images, work independently as well as collaboratively, and have an audience of not only a teacher and school peers within the walls of a classroom but a potentially larger audience as a result of online viewers.

So what exactly happened in this classroom? In this section, you'll get an overview of the visual nonfiction essay process, the technology students used (see Figures 1 and 2), and the how, the why, and the potential for making writing with technology matter to students.

Figure 1 *Process Overview*

**Reading and Discussing Historical Fiction**
    Selecting Texts
        Reading and Annotating Texts
            Logging Vocabulary and Historical References

**Reading and Researching: Creating Independent Projects**
    Reader Response: Independent Project

**Preparing to Research**
        Reading and Researching: Independent Projects

**Creating the Visual Nonfiction Essay**
    Selecting Topics
      Researching
        Storyboarding (and Researching Some More)
        Putting the Essay Together

Figure 2 *Technology Overview*

Conducting a WebQuest
Researching information and image sources online
Blogging
Analyzing electronic media messages
Using Microsoft Office PowerPoint
Editing with Microsoft Windows Movie Maker

# Chapter 5
# Reading and Discussing Historical Fiction

If students are to make a visual *nonfiction* essay, why read *fiction* books?

The beauty of historical fiction is that it blends fact and fiction and thereby engages students in story while humanizing some of the major topics and themes of the time periods that students learn about. Historical fiction exists for practically every time period students will read about. A few of our favorites are *My Brother Sam Is Dead* by James Lincoln Collier and Christopher Collier (American Revolution), *Out of the Dust* by Karen Hesse (Great Depression), *The Watsons Go to Birmingham—1963* by Christopher Paul Curtis (civil rights).

In this project, the teacher deliberately cast a wide net in order to represent the topics the students had learned about in the other content areas, from the feuding and raiding of the Medieval times to the art and culture of the Renaissance and Post-Renaissance. Teachers may choose to take on shorter periods of time or to select specific events and topics for students to research. Teachers can also work collaboratively with content-area teachers to time projects to coincide and support specific topics that students are studying in those classes.

In this chapter, we explain how and why students selected the texts they read as well as how annotating and noticing vocabulary and historical references helped students develop topics for research.

## Selecting Texts

Selecting books is an important decision because the texts need to be content-rich in a number of ways:

1. The content should address topics that are key to the time period(s) the students are studying.
2. The content should have ideas that give way to research.
3. The content should pique and sustain students' interest while they read the texts and beyond.

Consequently, the teacher needs to select a handful of historical fiction books. (See Figure 5.1 for summaries of the books selected for the Medieval to Post-Renaissance project.)

Figure 5.1 *Selected Historical Fiction Books*

<u>Medieval Times</u>
Farmer, N. 2004. *The Sea of Trolls*. New York: Simon & Schuster.

Two siblings, Jack, an eleven-year-old apprenticed to a Druid bard, and Lucy, a five-year-old who believes she is a princess, are captured by Viking berserkers and enslaved on a ship for countless months before arriving at the home of King Ivar the Boneless and his half-troll queen. Jack soon discovers his adventure is just beginning as he undertakes a quest to Jotunheim, home of the trolls, in an attempt to learn a magical spell in order to gain his and his sister's freedom.

Grant, K. M. 2004. *Blood Red Horse*. New York: Walker & Company.

Set during the time of the Third Crusade with England's King Richard I battling against the Muslim leader Saladin and his army, this story tells how one special horse alters the lives of two brothers, both soldiers and both in love with the same fair maiden.

Napoli, D. J. 2007. *Hush: An Irish Princess Tale*. New York: Atheneum.

Melkorka, a beautiful princess in Medieval Ireland, is kidnapped by Russian slave traders. Forced into slavery, she protects herself by taking a vow of silence, but soon realizes that her silence fascinates her captors, who believe she is enchanted.

<u>Renaissance and Post-Renaissance</u>
Blackwood, G. 2000. *Shakespeare Stealer*. New York: Penguin.

Widge, an orphan with street smarts and a talent for shorthand, is sent by his demanding master to steal Shakespeare's play *Hamlet*. The story takes an unexpected turn when Widge is accepted into the "family" of Globe Theater actors, and then realizes he would rather be an actor than a thief.

Cullen, L. 2007. *I Am Rembrandt's Daughter*. New York: Bloomsbury.

Set in Amsterdam in the 1600s, this novel weaves together the love story of Rembrandt's daughter, Cornelia, and the tragic story of the final years of Rembrandt's life, which he spent penniless and tottering on the brink of madness.

Konigsburg, E. L. 1975. *The Second Mrs. Gioconda*. New York: Simon & Schuster.

Leonardo da Vinci was one of the greatest artists of the Renaissance period. The inspiration for his famous painting, the *Mona Lisa*, is revealed as the story of Duchess Beatrice and da Vinci's trusted servant, Salai, unfolds.

Although teacher-led book talks are common in literacy classrooms, a WebQuest is an alternative that puts the onus on the students to discover what they might find interesting about a book. A WebQuest is an inquiry-oriented activity in which students gain information about books from web sources. Teachers do the initial planning for a WebQuest by locating online sources that provide information about the preselected texts. These sources can include official author websites, book review sites, and bookseller sites such as Barnes and Noble and Amazon. Teachers review the content within these sites to check for age-level appropriateness; they might also need to ensure that the sites are approved—not blocked or censored—by the school district. Teachers should then compile a list of the links that they will provide students. (See Appendix B: "Handout: Conducting a WebQuest" to use while guiding your students as they complete the WebQuest.)

For time efficiency, consider a jigsaw approach in which small groups of students research a particular book and then share their WebQuest findings with the whole class. Because these books are intended to generate possible research topics, students should include in their presentations an explanation of the historical events that are the foundation of each book. For instance, in *The Sea of Trolls* (Farmer 2006), the author depicts the raiding and viciousness of the Vikings, while in *I Am Rembrandt's Daughter* (Cullen 2007), the author explores the change in Rembrandt's artistic style late in his career.

Students then individually select a text that matches their interest(s). For example, Melissa said about her selection, "I chose *I Am Rembrandt's Daughter* because I like art and love stories," and several boys flocked to *Blood Red Horse* (Grant 2004) when they learned that the book promised to be packed with action and adventure.

## Reading and Annotating Texts

As students read their books, they need opportunities to share their thoughts and feelings as well as their puzzlements. Literature circle groups (ideally about four or five members each) can be formed based on common book selections. Teachers need to plan and announce a schedule of reading times and meeting times. Students need to prepare for each meeting time by reading an agreed-upon number of pages; marking (with highlighters or sticky notes) places in the text that interest them and adding margin notes; and writing out questions they want to discuss with their group. For example, after reading Chapter 1 of *I Am Rembrandt's Daughter*, Teresa marked the sentence "The van Loos would never have him [Cornelia's brother], poor as we are" (Cullen 2007, 12) and wrote the question, *If Cornelia's family is related to the van Loos, why is her family so much poorer?* When Teresa brought up this question, the answer led to a discussion of the class system, an issue explored in the book.

As another example, Teresa marked and connected two pieces of text that show the author is portraying Cornelia as insecure:

> And he could be gazing back at them, his mind far from the unkempt daughter of a failed doodler . . . (Cullen 2007, 134)
>
> I could perform with all the comportment in the world and still not compete with a rich merchant's pretty daughter. He had said he liked me. But why would he? (Narration by Cornelia) (Cullen 2007, 134)

Teresa's annotation in the left margin was *self-esteem*. Here, she responded as an engaged reader of story, fascinated by how the author characterized Cornelia as unkempt and unworthy. Annotating the text in such a way means that each student will have something to bring up for discussion at the next literature circle meeting.

The rich discussions that often occur in the literature circles have important effects: They not only help students understand on a deeper level the major themes and ideas in the texts, but also enable students to home in on the ideas that they want to know more about. For example, Teresa's highlighted sections relate to the art concepts that she picked up on and discussed with her group (see Figure 5.2). For Teresa and many of the students in the class, these annotations and discussions subsequently influenced the topic of their research.

Figure 5.2 *Teresa's Highlighted Nonfiction Sections*

| | |
|---|---|
| "'Light against darkness, the first principle of painting. What is light without darkness to set it off? Same goes for joy and pain. How are you to savor joy if you have never known pain?'" (Rembrandt to Cornelia, p. 66) | Teresa found this to be an important nonfiction detail about art, one she researched later. |
| "'What you call 'twisting,' Neel says, 'we painters call *contrapposto*.'" . . . "'Leonardo da Vinci used it in all his works. He thought that arranging his figures on a curving axis added life to his compositions.'" (p. 74) | Teresa circled the word *contrapposto*, an art term, and highlighted the sentence that expanded on it. |
| "'How else would you explain the truth of emotion in that picture? Is it so impossible for God to have guided him [Rembrandt]? Have you another explanation?'" (Neel to Cornelia, p. 105) | Teresa was drawn to details about Rembrandt's art that the author subtly wove into the text. |

# Logging Vocabulary and Historical References

Keeping track of vocabulary and historical references is another way to help students attend to nonfiction aspects of the historical fiction texts. Using a simple framework, students can log new, unusual, or interesting uses of words and phrases, the page number, and the meaning or significance. (See Appendix B: "Handout: Vocabulary and Historical References Log.") In addition, readers of historical fiction will come across historical events and/or people who are connected to the time period. Students can draw from this list of historical references and/or the context-specific vocabulary as they pursue their research.

A review of many students' logs showed that the students in this project noted the nonfiction vocabulary that helped build background knowledge of the topics, concepts, and themes that eventually found their way into their visual nonfiction essays. For example, Adrian, who read *Blood Red Horse* (Grant 2004) about the Crusades, made notes of words like *sapper* (a soldier), *imam* (the governor of a Muslim city), *sultan* (the leader of a Muslim kingdom), and *arbalesters* (Medieval crossbows). When it was time for Adrian to consider research topics, he scanned his list and noticed that these words related to Muslim warriors. Obviously, as Adrian read, he was interested in this "category" of words, if you will. It was no surprise, then, that in his visual nonfiction essay, Adrian addressed many aspects of the Muslim warriors involved in the Crusades.

*Engagement*

■ ■ ■ ■ ■

All in all, reading historical fiction can attract students to the topics and themes of the time period(s) being researched. (See Figure 5.3 for the key points of beginning with reading.) Even reluctant readers of nonfiction are able to use historical fiction novels to find topics that interest them. Students' margin notes, literature circle discussions, and vocabulary and historical references logs all pave the way for students' research.

Figure 5.3 (part 1) *Why Begin with Reading?*

---

**Why Begin with Reading?**

- Use reading to get students ready for nonfiction study. Mrs. Newstead said, "I use reading to get students invested in the research and writing." Arial shared that she put in a lot of effort [into her research projects] because she felt a connection to her topic.
- Select books that seamlessly integrate factual information into interesting stories. Arial selected a text that "contained mystery and art history."

---

**Figure 5.3 (part2)** *Why Begin with Reading?*

- Select books that appeal to students' interests. Teresa wrote, *I am not a big fan of history, so I wanted a love story to go along with it.*
- Use historical fiction to interest reluctant readers and writers of nonfiction. Allison wrote, *I usually read fiction novels only, and I like creative writing. This project helped me expand my horizons into nonfiction. I learned that it is fun to do a nonfiction project.*
- Use historical fiction to give a human perspective to events of the past. Adrian wrote, *There are many things that happened in this book [Blood Red Horse] that could be lost and forgotten. It puts a new face on the object or person in the book.*
- Use reading to build background knowledge of the topics, themes, and time periods that students will research.
- Use historical fiction to develop students as "noticers" of vocabulary and historical references that are authentic to the contexts.

# Chapter 6
# Reading and Researching: Creating Independent Projects

After reading and annotating historical fiction, discussing in literature circles, and logging vocabulary and historical references, students will have collected many ideas that interest them.

Students are then ready to explore some of those ideas further by creating independent projects. They need the opportunity to work independently to think about, form ideas about, and respond to the concepts that intrigued them as they read and discussed the historical fiction. This thinking work will then serve as the basis for the content of the visual nonfiction essay that they'll construct collaboratively with their peers.

The independent projects are divided into two categories, reader response and reading and researching (see Figure 6.1). In both types of projects, students present the information creatively in a variety of genres and forms. To complete the reader response projects, students can stay mostly within the pages of the historical fiction texts. For example, students can synthesize the information they marked and discussed while reading the historical fiction in order to create a dramatic monologue or craft an alternative ending. To complete the reading and researching projects, students need to extend beyond the pages of the historical fiction texts by conducting research about the ideas related to the time periods that they marked and discussed. For example, students who choose to assemble an A-to-Z book or design a web page will need to turn to additional sources to find the information they need.

Figure 6.1 *Independent Project Choices*

| Reader Response | Reading and Researching |
|---|---|
| Alternative endings | Articles/newsletters |
| Book trailers/advertisements | A-to-Z books |
| Cartoons | Brochures |
| Chapter after the end | Book covers |
| Character diaries/ | Editorials |
| memoirs/letters | Interviews |
| Dramatic monologues | Maps |
| Editorials | Newspapers |
| Parodies | Parodies |
| Picture books | Picture books |
| Poetry | Reviews |
| Reviews | Research essays |
| Time lines | Web pages |

The structure of this phase of the project is loose as students work mostly independently and the teacher acts as a facilitator and holds short, informal conferences with students to check on progress. Teachers may decide to treat each project separately and have students complete the reader response project first before introducing the reading and researching project. Or they may present students with both project assignments and allow students to work on both simultaneously. Whatever the case, before students begin the reading and researching project, a few mini-lessons about the research process are essential. Students need to understand the importance of finding credible sources, verifying information, and citing sources to avoid plagiarism. (See Appendix B: "Activity: Credibility of Sources"; "Activity: Verifying Information"; "Activity: Avoiding Plagiarism.") As students begin their research, they will also need to learn to keep track of the sources they consult. (See Appendix B: "Handout: Tracking Electronic and Print Sources.")

In this chapter, we first display some of the projects and highlight interesting features. Then we discuss the benefits of allowing students to work individually as readers, researchers, and writers.

## Reviewing the Students' Independent Projects

Here are several individual projects and the distinctive ways students approached them.

### Alternative Endings

Ramon explained his process for crafting an alternative ending to *The Second Mrs. Gioconda* (Konigsburg 1975):

> I went back and reviewed the last chapter before I began writing this alternative ending to see how the author laid out everything.

Ramon also detailed what he wanted to preserve as well as what he wanted to change. (See Figure 6.2.)

> The author leaves you hanging, and I wanted to write an ending that did that too. But in my ending, I made Leonardo's personality different because in the book, he was sympathetic [to Salai's victims], and I thought that made him kind of boring.

Figure 6.2 *Ramon's Alternative Ending*

---

## Alternative Ending to The Second Mrs. Gioconda

"So," Mr. Gioconda said, "Mr. Leonardo will paint a portrait of my wife?" "Oh definitely, of course," Salai replied with a sneer, for Salai knew this would be a quick buck and an easy steal. "Let me go consult with Master Leonardo," said Salai. Salai left the room and went to his bed to think things through. What his scheme will be this time, he wondered. His old knife? No, too old of a trick. He needed more of a challenge . He knew this was a merchant, a master at the art of pick pocketing. He would need a devious plot to sneak around him. An idea then struck his mind as he was fetching his Master.

"Yes, what would you like-hurry please, I'm a very busy man!" Leonardo said as he and Salai walked in together. "Yes I sir, I would like you to make a portrait of my lovely wife, Madonna Lisa, or Mona Lisa as people call her." Mr. Gioconda said. "Hmm... no, I am man of the great fine arts and too busy for some peasants wife," declared Leonardo almost as it was an insult. Then it hit him. What would people's reactions be if they saw this painting? It was a clever thought, an original idea. As The Giocondas were about to exit the studio, Da Vinci stopped them and said, "Wait! I agree to your offer," said Leonardo, now with more acceptance. "Oh thank you Monsieur Leonardo, thank you!" exclaimed Mr. Gioconda, "So I presume 50 scudis?" "Yes, that'll be fine," replied Leonardo. This entire time Salai was conjuring up a plot. And he knew what it was going to be. "Then it's a deal!" Mr. Gioconda said. "Please, let me show you the exit." Leonardo said.

"Not bad of a deal, 50 scudis," Leonardo said when he returned. "Not bad at all, Master," Salai responded, "but, wouldn't 100 scudis be better?" "Well of course, Salai, but why say something so preposterous when we only are receiving-" Salai flashed his stolen 50 scudis in front of Leonardo's face. Usually Da Vinci was a honest man, but suddenly changed his expression with a half smile, "Very impressive, Salai," Leonardo said in amazement, "But not good enough" he replied with a sneer."

---

# Poetry

Excerpts from two students' poetry showed experimentation with rhythm and repetition, synthesis of the themes and conflicts in historical fiction texts, and the incorporation of vocabulary logged during their reading. Allison's "Hush Poem" was enhanced by ending each stanza with the line "I must hush." (See Figure 6.3.) Emelia's poem "Why Hush?" explained that the answer to this question saved the main character's life. (See Figure 6.4.)

Figure 6.3 *"Hush Poem" by Allison*

**Hush Poem**

Taken. My royal life torn away,
Onto a slave ship is where I now reside,
with no one to trust by my side.
I must hush.

My whole world is spinning:
this is surely the end.
I can't even try to pretend that I am back home.
I must hush.

But amongst this terror, this fear, I remain silent.
Hush.
If I hush I will become a mystery, an enigma to solve,
and the torture that was near will disappear.
I must hush.

Overboard she jumps, my delicate sister, Bridgid
she plunges into the water so frigid.
My heart stops. My very soul is severed.
I must hush.

I am no longer princess Melkorka,
but Aist. A stork they tell me.
A mystic being they believe.
This is not me.
What has happened?
I must hush.

Figure 6.4 (part 1) *"Why Hush?" by Emelia*

**Why Hush?**

Being silent seems like a challenge
That is silly to take on.
"For what is the purpose?"
I ask my mother with a yawn.

"It will protect you."
Her once-controlled mask slips without a notion,
And just for an instant
I can read her true emotion.

We, her precious, beloved children,
Her only heirs to the Irish throne,
May get harassed, hurt, or murdered;
We may never come home.

Figure 6.4 (part 2) *"Why Hush?" by Emelia*

I am now gazing out at the night sky on a ship of immense and absolute terror.
A tear trickles down my cheek as my hands cling harder to the rail,
Wanting to throw myself overboard
For now I am a proell.

I pertain the lowest amount of rights,
Of any social class on this whole Earth.
I may even be lowlier than our old, useless dog,
Whose greatest comfort was sleeping on the iron-hard stone by the hearth.

For I come from a castle
Of powerful Irish reign.
I am blue blood at heart
Who has never suffered the slightest amount of pain.

## Time Lines

Designing time lines appeals to students who think visually and who like information organized systematically. Adrian's novel approach to constructing a time line allowed him to document how two characters figured into the main plot line of *Blood Red Horse* (Grant 2004). (See Figure 6.5.) Because *Blood Red Horse* is not told chronologically, Sergio had to return again and again to the text to carefully plot and match the main events and dates. (See Figure 6.6.) Notice the amount of writing and level of detail in both time lines.

Figure 6.5 *Adrian's Time Line*

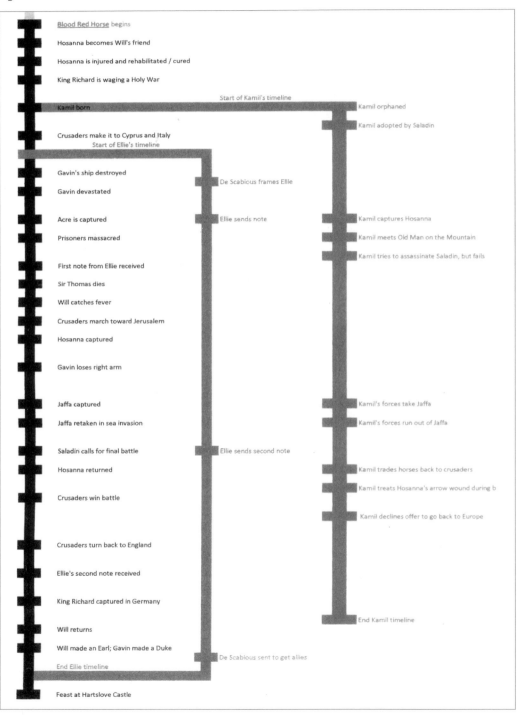

Blood Red Horse begins

Hosanna becomes Will's friend

Hosanna is injured and rehabilitated / cured

King Richard is waging a Holy War

Start of Kamil's timeline                    Kamil orphaned

Kamil born                                   Kamil adopted by Saladin

Crusaders make it to Cyprus and Italy
Start of Ellie's timeline

Gavin's ship destroyed          De Scabious frames Ellie

Gavin devastated

Acre is captured                Ellie sends note          Kamil captures Hosanna

Prisoners massacred                                       Kamil meets Old Man on the Mountain

                                                          Kamil tries to assassinate Saladin, but fails

First note from Ellie received

Sir Thomas dies

Will catches fever

Crusaders march toward Jerusalem

Hosanna captured

Gavin loses right arm

Jaffa captured                                            Kamil's forces take Jaffa

Jaffa retaken in sea invasion                             Kamil's forces run out of Jaffa

Saladin calls for final battle    Ellie sends second note

Hosanna returned                                          Kamil trades horses back to crusaders

                                                          Kamil treats Hosanna's arrow wound during b

Crusaders win battle                                      Kamil declines offer to go back to Europe

Crusaders turn back to England

Ellie's second note received

King Richard captured in Germany

Will returns                                              End Kamil timeline

Will made an Earl; Gavin made a Duke    De Scabious sent to get allies

End Ellie timeline

Feast at Hartslove Castle

Figure 6.6 *Sergio's Time Line*

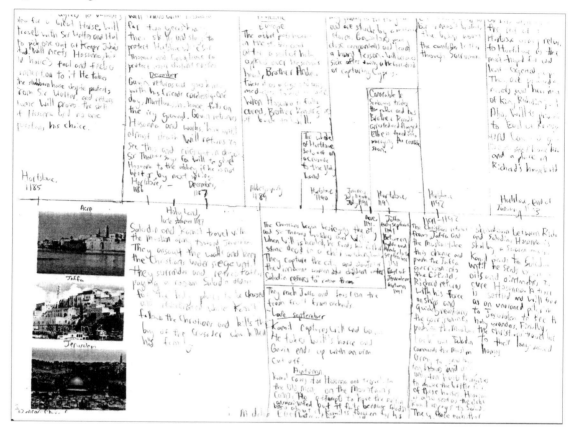

## A-to-Z Books

Melissa talked about choosing this project: "I had some ideas from my reading, and an A-to-Z book is different from a research paper and I liked putting [the information] together like this." For the letter *D*, Death, Melissa explained, "I chose the image of a mass burial because the picture represents that there were so many deaths, they couldn't bury the people by themselves." On one page, Melissa pulled information from a history textbook and related it to the historical fiction text she read. Melissa also recognized that an A-to-Z book required pairing images with ideas, adding a dimension not found in traditional research papers. (See Figure 6.7.)

Figure 6.7 *A Page from Melissa's A-to-Z Book*

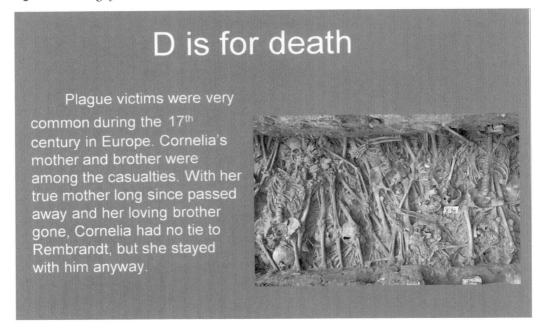

## Newspaper Articles

Connor adopted the format of a newspaper with his masthead, titles, two-column text, an "In this issue" preview box, and images. Connor's articles were a synthesis of information from *The Sea of Trolls* (Farmer 2006), print and online sources, and his own clever ideas. (See Figure 6.8.)

## Parodies

Parodying the style of survival books such as *The Boys' Book of Survival: How to Survive Anything Anywhere* (Campbell 2009), Chad explored how to survive Northmen raids. Chad said, "I thought maybe I would make an [informational] article. I started by playing around by drawing out some pictures. Then I remembered reading a book about the chances of surviving this or that. And then I started writing what the chances of survival would be." In the end, Chad presented content information in a creative form. (See Figure 6.9.)

Figure 6.8 *The First Page of Connor's Newspaper*

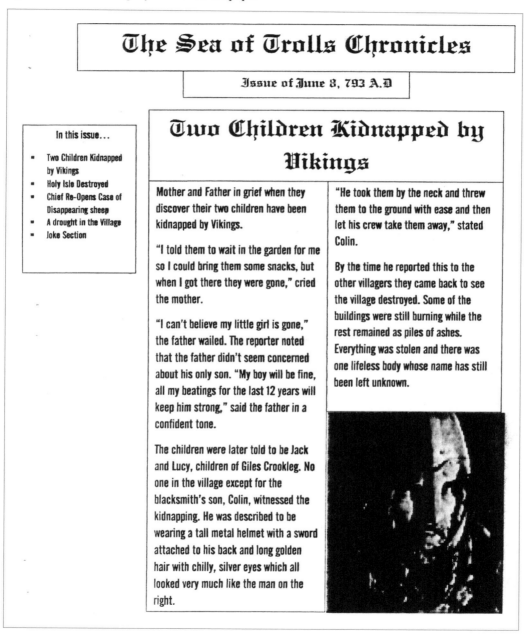

# The Sea of Trolls Chronicles

Issue of June 8, 793 A.D

**In this issue...**

- Two Children Kidnapped by Vikings
- Holy Isle Destroyed
- Chief Re-Opens Case of Disappearing sheep
- A drought in the Village
- Joke Section

## Two Children Kidnapped by Vikings

Mother and Father in grief when they discover their two children have been kidnapped by Vikings.

"I told them to wait in the garden for me so I could bring them some snacks, but when I got there they were gone," cried the mother.

"I can't believe my little girl is gone," the father wailed. The reporter noted that the father didn't seem concerned about his only son. "My boy will be fine, all my beatings for the last 12 years will keep him strong," said the father in a confident tone.

The children were later told to be Jack and Lucy, children of Giles Crookleg. No one in the village except for the blacksmith's son, Colin, witnessed the kidnapping. He was described to be wearing a tall metal helmet with a sword attached to his back and long golden hair with chilly, silver eyes which all looked very much like the man on the right.

"He took them by the neck and threw them to the ground with ease and then let his crew take them away," stated Colin.

By the time he reported this to the other villagers they came back to see the village destroyed. Some of the buildings were still burning while the rest remained as piles of ashes. Everything was stolen and there was one lifeless body whose name has still been left unknown.

Figure 6.9 *Chad's Parody of a Survival Book*

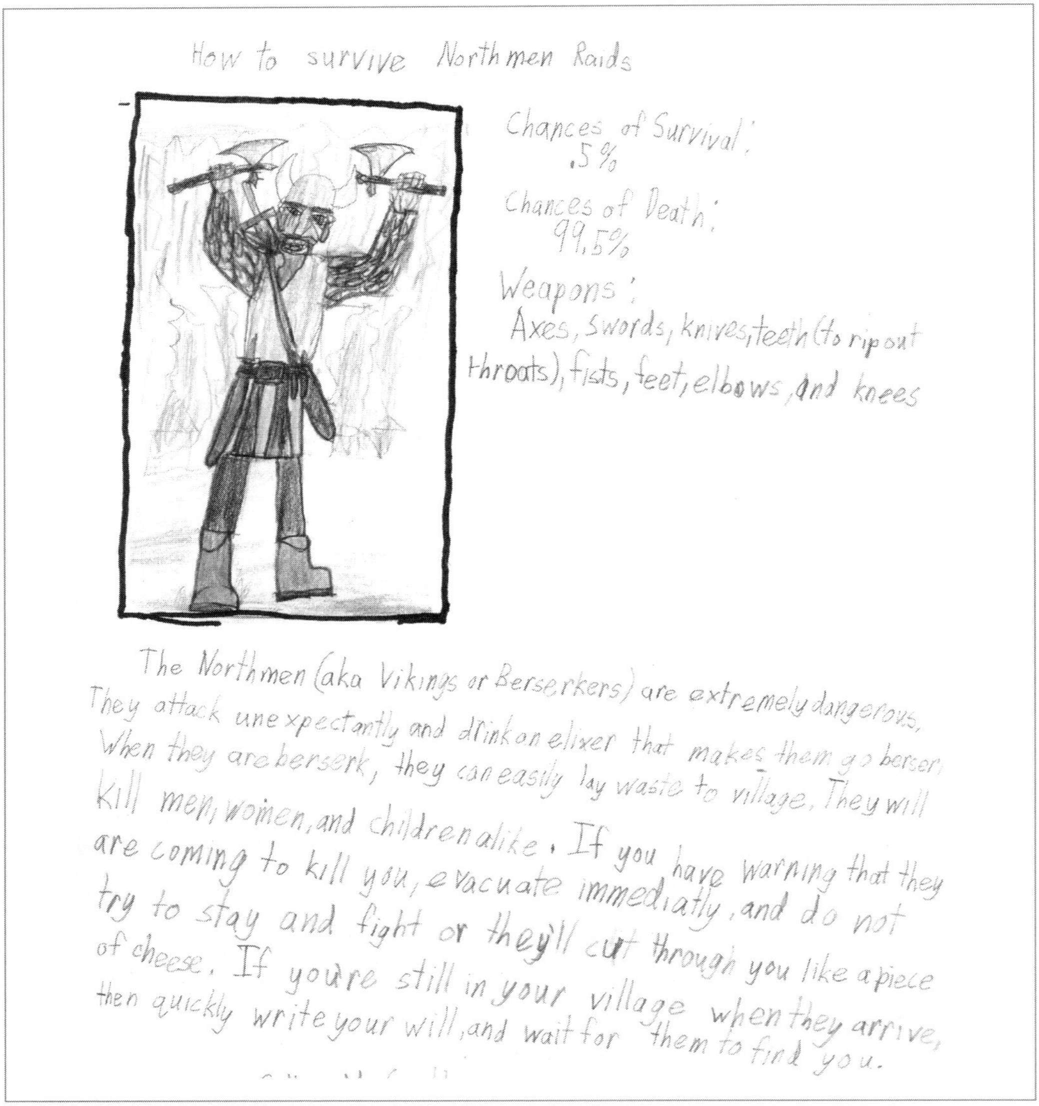

How to survive Northmen Raids

Chances of Survival:
.5%

Chances of Death:
99.5%

Weapons:
Axes, Swords, knives, teeth (to rip out throats), fists, feet, elbows, and knees

The Northmen (aka Vikings or Berserkers) are extremely dangerous. They attack unexpectantly and drink an elixer that makes them go berserk. When they are berserk, they can easily lay waste to village. They will kill men, women, and children alike. If you have warning that they are coming to kill you, evacuate immediatly, and do not try to stay and fight or they'll cut through you like a piece of cheese. If you're still in your village when they arrive, then quickly write your will, and wait for them to find you.

## Reviews

In an early draft of her review of the *Mona Lisa*, Arial, drawing on her background knowledge of art and art reviews as a genre, commented on many features of the painting. (See Figure 6.10.)

Figure 6.10 *Arial's Art Review Draft of the* Mona Lisa

---

**Response to the Mona Lisa**

When I first look at the 'Mona Lisa', I notice the intriguing look on her face. The expression is one that reminds me of a lady that is neither happy nor sad, neither smiling nor frowning. Her skin is very smooth and she has no blemishes, but also she has no eyebrows, which makes her look quite strange.

At different times the expression on Mona Lisa changes. Sometimes she is giving a cheeky smile and others she looks puzzled. This is very strange and almost magical. Also, when looking at the Mona Lisa, I notice that her face is bathed in light. This light is almost heavenly and gives the impression that she is angelic. But on the contrary, another thing I notice is the dark clothing and gloomy mysterious background setting. The dark clothing and the veil covering her hair give the impression that she has been to a funeral or is in mourning.

The background setting is very mysterious. The winding roads, ravenous mountains and the gloomy fog all add to the mystery. It is as if the background is right out of a fantasy story. Another weird thing that the background does is makes the beholder unsure on which time of day it is in the picture. The Mona Lisa is a mystical painting, and because of its magic, it is considered one of, if not the most renowned painting of our times. There is also the mystery of why Leonardo painted her, a simple merchants wife. There are many stories and tales about why, one of them 'The Second Mrs. Giaconda,' but no one is really sure. This fact also contributes to the unexplained magic to this grand painting.

---

# The Value of Independent Projects

Why have students complete individual projects? Here are four ways in which the process was valuable to students.

## 1. The research is multisourced.

Reading the historical fiction texts provides students with intriguing ideas that can serve as the basis for further exploration with independent projects. In order to complete independent projects, students will need to do research to flesh out their ideas. As students build a bank of knowledge, they will weave together information from multiple sources.

Research

During an interview, Patrick, working with a first draft, talked us through the information contained in the second paragraph, shown below, of his research essay titled "The Pros and Cons of the Third Crusade":

> There were many negative things that made this crusade one to remember. The major goal of the Christians was to get Jerusalem back from the Muslims, but that didn't happen. For the Christians, this is the worst thing that could happen. They felt like they had lost and that the whole crusade was a waste of time. The most horrific thing that came out of the crusade was that many lives were lost. In one battle alone, King Richard killed 2,700 Muslims, and Saladin responded by killing all the Christian prisoners. All the bloodshed was just terrible. Also, during the crusade, the church either sold or gave the nobles' land back home to priests and clergymen. The worst part of it all was that the crusaders were fighting and risking their lives for the church, and then the church took their land. All of these things made this a horrific crusade.

Patrick explained his source identification process:

*I got that King Richard was a strategist and that he really led [the Crusades] more from the book [Blood Red Horse]. That the Christians lost to the Muslims, I got from Encarta. The church either sold or gave the noble's land back to priests and clergymen, I got that from [Blood Red Horse]. That they felt that the crusade was a waste of time, I got from Encyclopedia Britannica.*

Patrick is not overly dependent on a particular source, and he seamlessly integrates information from several sources to make his points. It is likely that his nonfiction knowledge gained from reading *Blood Red Horse* gave him the necessary context and major themes and ideas to which he could attach new details and events he was learning as he read from *Encyclopedia Britannica* and other sources.

The research essay and other project choices involving reading and researching require students to gather and synthesize information from multiple sources.

## 2. The research emerges organically.

Tasking students to write in particular genres means that they might need to seek more content knowledge in order to support and elaborate their ideas.

Melissa's decision to create an A-to-Z book meant that she had to find twenty-six ideas or topics that represented the historical fiction novel *I Am Rembrandt's Daughter* (Cullen 2007). To do so, she combed through the book and plucked out many of the nonfiction elements within this fictional text, looked to her annotations for important ideas, and used her vocabulary and historical references log to plan out an idea or topic for each letter.

Melissa revealed that the task required a great deal of negotiation. For instance, for the letter *A*, she said, "I was thinking about *A Is for Art* but thought I would do *P Is for Paintings* instead. I decided *A Is for Amsterdam* is better because without the setting, you can't visualize [the story]."

*Critical Thinking*

But a quality A-to-Z book is not a matter of identifying one word or idea for each letter. To flesh out her ideas, Melissa went in search of additional information and images she could add. She stated, "For the information I wrote, I would sometimes summarize a scene . . . or read information online . . . or I would try to locate more information, like dates, for certain paintings." Melissa also used a Google search to locate images that would match the text she had written.

*Research*

Melissa culled information from multiple sources to provide relevant information that supported *P Is for Paintings*. (See Figure 6.11.) Essentially she presented three ideas:

Figure 6.11 *Melissa's* P is for Paintings *Page*

## P is for paintings

Rembrandt had a special painting technique for which he was and is known. He always used lots of dark colors to make the brighter colors stand out. He is mostly famous for his portraits. Rembrandt made over 100 paintings, and there are 41 etchings, 37 self-portraits, and 70 drawings!

Rembrandt had a particular style of contrasting dark and light images, he was known for painting portraits, and he had a number of artworks to his credit. Interestingly, Melissa included and elaborated on all of these ideas in her group's visual nonfiction essay.

## 3. The independent projects span multiple genres.

Genre Learning

A variety of projects allows students to write across fiction and nonfiction genres and brings about new learning. Learning in both content and genre knowledge occurs as students take a body of knowledge and shape it in new ways, depending on the type of project the students select.

Allison's decision to take the rich story of the 308-page book *Hush: An Irish Princess Tale* (Napoli 2007) and mold it into a short poem necessitated that she synthesize the major events of the story, determine a narrow focus for the poem, and develop a structure and presentation style.

Sergio's decision to create a time line for the text *Blood Red Horse* (Grant 2004) required that he represent the major events in a visual way. He departed from a traditional one-line diagram because he wanted also to document how the two main characters figured into the events, ultimately creating a time line with much complexity.

Critical Thinking

The process of shaping the data in new ways, for new genres, required Allison and Sergio to return repeatedly to their historical fiction books for information and details about characters and the sequence of events. Simultaneously, these students worked to depict the story accurately while contending with the features of the new text, such as rhythm and repetition for poetry, and linear and concise depiction of information for time lines. Other projects required students to draw on models for content, language, structure, features, style, and tone in order to represent the genres authentically.

## 4. The independent projects invite creativity.

Shaping information in new structures allows space for creativity.

Connor created *The Sea of Trolls Chronicles*, a newspaper in which he showcased his genre and content knowledge as well as his sense of humor. The newspaper featured illustrated news articles, an "In this issue" sidebar, and a joke section.

Two of Connor's news articles depicted several main events in the book *The Sea of Trolls* (Farmer 2006), including Viking kidnappings and the destruction of the Holy Isle. Connor drew the information for the news articles from details in the book ("Giles Grookleg's two children were kidnapped by the raiding Vikings"), from researched information ("the manuscripts were shredded and the bibles burned"), and his own imagination ("no one in the village except for the blacksmith's son, Colin, witnessed the kidnapping"). In another article, "Chief Re-Opens Case of Disappearing Sheep," Connor expanded one small detail in the book—that sheep are herded—into an article that included humorous statements such as, "last night twenty sheep were stolen . . . and villagers are worried that this will lead to a lamb chop shortage." Connor continued to capitalize on humor by including a joke section replete with jokes that include time-period references to barbarians, monks, trolls, and berserkers. All told, the newspaper format allowed Connor to merge facts, fiction, and images in a creative way.

Chad's decision to tackle a parody meant that he had to find a text format that he could parody and analyze as a model, and into which he could incorporate humor and sarcasm when synthesizing researched information based on the book *The Sea of Trolls* (Farmer 2006). (Refer back to page 60 for Chad's parody.) In his parody, Chad drew from a popular nonfiction text (*The Boys' Book of Survival: How to Survive Anything Anywhere* [Campbell 2009]) in which he provided readers with advice about how to survive difficult situations. Sarcasm abounded in every section of Chad's advice on "How to Survive Northmen Raids." Chad informed readers that their chances of survival were .5 percent, which is not good by any standard. He also advised readers to use every available weapon, including "teeth (to rip out throats), fists, feet, elbows, and knees," but one look at the image Chad provided of a Viking warrior told readers that such weapons were quite inferior. In the running text, Chad advised that readers should "evacuate immediately . . . and not try to stay and fight or [the Northmen will] cut through you like a piece of cheese"; another option he offered was to "quickly write your will and wait for them to find you."

All of these are examples of how Chad has adopted the nature and tone of parody and applied it to the context of surviving a Northmen raid. Chad integrated researched information without distracting from the humor. He pointed out that Northmen "attack unexpectedly," "drink an elixir that makes them go berserk," "can lay waste to village" under the influence of the elixir, and "will kill men, women, and children alike." This factual information actually underscored the information that Chad presented more sarcastically, such as that the chances of survival might as well have been zero and that trying to fight the warriors was pretty much futile.

The independent projects that students took on were challenging because they were not fact-filled, humdrum summaries from a single source. Instead, students were required to think critically about texts, sharpen their research and analysis skills, try on genre features, and synthesize information, all the while creating the space they needed to show their creativity. The open-ended design of the project allowed the teacher to guide a range of independent projects that empowered students to pursue their interests and talents without having to stick to a predetermined framework.

Taken as a whole, these independent projects cause students to work on many levels. As students begin researching, they soon find themselves jumping from fiction to nonfiction sources, from print sources to online sources, from print to images, from prose to poetry, and from the familiar to the new.

At the heart of the independent projects is that students have the opportunity to work from their personal interests while taking on the challenge of writing texts in multiple genres, which often requires both content and genre research.

Steeped in the time periods being studied, students are then ready to rejoin their peers and use their ideas as the basis for creating a visual nonfiction essay.

# Chapter 7
# Creating the Visual Nonfiction Essay

By completing their independent projects, students expanded their knowledge through reading and researching and had something to bring to the table when it was time to begin the group projects—producing visual nonfiction essays.

A group project. Fun.

A group project involving computers. More fun.

Students may want to storm the technology lab, download Windows Movie Maker, and get going.

To help them understand exactly what they will be constructing together, use a rubric to explain the research, writing, and production components of a visual nonfiction essay. (See Appendix B: "Visual Nonfiction Essay Rubric: Research/Writing Aspects" and "Visual Nonfiction Essay Rubric: Production Aspects.")

In this chapter, we discuss the process the students will follow in order to create the visual nonfiction essay: selecting topics, researching, storyboarding, and producing the visual nonfiction essay.

## Selecting Topics

Process

Selecting topics is the first step toward creating the visual nonfiction essay. Because these essays are constructed collaboratively, students should return to their original literature circle groups. Have the students begin by sharing their independent projects. Doing so will get the groups buzzing with ideas.

To help students think about how to corral their ideas and make an appropriate topic selection, present them with a few criteria for the visual nonfiction essay. For example, a visual nonfiction essay presents content that

- can be covered sufficiently in a short time frame;
- is suited to a visual medium; and
- has audience appeal.

With criteria in view, students can then try to sell their ideas in their literature circle groups. In one group, five students explored topic ideas inspired by their reading of *I Am Rembrandt's Daughter* (Cullen 2007):

**Jessica:** We could do the plague.

**Teresa:** We could research Rembrandt's paintings.

**Catherine:** The plague is kind of broad.

**Jessica:** We can change it up.

**Evelyn:** Well, I did my personal research project on the plague.

**Jessica:** Me too.

**Teresa:** If we do the paintings, we'll have to do a small selection of them.

**Melissa:** He was a popular artist and everyone loved him and then he changed the way of doing things.

**Catherine:** We could write about Amsterdam.

**Evelyn:** Amsterdam is too broad. I don't know about that.

**Jessica:** I like the bubonic plague.

**Melissa:** It is not going to be very long.

**Catherine:** It is going to be a video.

**Teresa:** We need to make something that we can see.

*Collaboration*

In this short exchange, three ideas—the plague, Rembrandt's paintings, Amsterdam—were tossed in for consideration and were immediately evaluated for their potential as research topics. Catherine seemingly dismissed an idea by saying "the plague is kind of broad," but because Jessica and Evelyn had researched the topic for their independent projects, they defended the idea as a viable one. Picking up on the criteria that the topics must be narrow, Teresa said, "If we do the paintings, we'll have to do a small selection of them" and Melissa added information to bolster Teresa's idea that Rembrandt's paintings could be a strong topic. The discussion about the need for a narrow topic led the group to consider the length of the final product. Melissa reminded the group, "It is not going to be very long." Then Teresa homed in on an important feature of a video: "We need to make something that we can see." From this discussion, the group recognized that they needed to select a topic that met the criteria for a visual nonfiction essay.

To extend the discussion and open it to a larger audience, teachers can have students share their selected topic by posting it on a class blog for other class members to respond to. A few sentence starters will help students share their ideas (see below; see also Appendix B: "Handout: Topic Rationale and Blog Response Questions"):

Our topic is _____.

We selected this topic because _____
_____.

We plan to cover these major ideas: _____
_____.

We still have these questions: _____
_____.

Responders should be encouraged to provide feedback and suggestions about the topic, possible resources, and the potential topic appeal to the audience. Consider asking responders to address one or more of these questions:

- What aspect(s) about this topic appeals to you?
- Do you know of any resources this group can consult?
- Can you address or answer any of the group's questions?
- Do you have an idea that the group should consider?

Group members can then read the postings and meet together to reevaluate and finalize their topics.

All in all, selecting a topic for research in a collaborative group allows students to draw upon the content and genre knowledge they have acquired from their independent projects and to jockey for their ideas to be valued. In these discussions, both face-to-face and virtually, students address the desired qualities of a visual nonfiction essay, and these criteria shape the topics to pursue.

## Researching

Teacher Disposition

After selecting a topic, the next step is research, a continuation of the process students engaged in while completing their independent projects. As a result, students should be able to work collaboratively with limited oversight. Teachers move from group to group, listen in on students' conversations about their research, and provide content and technical assistance as needed. Teachers may also want to provide a review of the critical aspects of research, such as citing and tracking sources.

The twenty-first-century student gravitates toward researching electronically because it allows users to access information easily. As a result, researchers cover more content more quickly. During this project, a group of boys sat side by side using computers to dig deeper into their research:

> **Sergio:** Let's search *Crusades*.
> **Keith:** All the sources are not anything like our books.
> **Adrian:** There's nothing on this website.
> **Sergio:** Well, get on another one. I'm going to look at *Encarta*.
> **Keith:** Here, look, we can look at Saladin right here.
> **Sergio:** Look up *Crusades*, and I will look up *Saladin*.
> **Patrick:** What are you looking at?
> **Adrian:** This website has information on tactics.

In a matter of minutes, these students juggled three topics—the Crusades, Saladin, and tactics—and when one website did not provide information judged useful by them, they moved on and had more information within seconds.

Students found that there were many online sources to help them flesh out their focused topics. For instance, Teresa commented, "I used Wikipedia because it had a lot of different [sub]topics on the plague." Keith, too, found that Wikipedia was helpful in that it "had good description on the knights, horses, and equipment." Sergio wrote, "I used *Encyclopedia Britannica* because it gave me a variety of information and pictures." The students found that research databases such as these provided lengthy overviews on topics, often organized with subheadings, and that they could quickly navigate the content to find information related to their topics.

Students in this project also found that they had to be critical readers when digging into sources. They could heed only the information that would support their focused topic. Sergio, who was studying the Crusades, soon discovered that "much of the information on the actual Crusades was unhelpful since my group was researching the weapons and armor used back then." Although Sergio could have become overwhelmed by the amount of information that was available on the Crusades, he had narrowed his topic beforehand and was able to navigate the sources in search of information that related to weapons and armor.

Researching was important to this project because it allowed students to build the content knowledge that they would need to create the visual nonfiction essay. At the same time, though, students increased their knowledge of the research process. They learned to access and synthesize information from multiple sources and to question the accuracy and usefulness of the content. These skills are vital for twenty-first-century students who have to navigate the ever-increasing body of knowledge that is available to them as a result of technology.

## Storyboarding

Once students have amassed a considerable amount of content knowledge on their topics, the groups are ready to decide how best to organize and present their ideas.

Enter storyboards. A storyboard consists of a set of boxes in which a writer places text, pictures, and symbols. Storyboarding looks deceptively simple—it seems as though a writer merely plans the information sequentially from start to finish. However, along the way, the writer is making both text and image-based decisions: What information should or should not be included? How should details be conveyed, as text or as pictures? What level of detail is needed to convey the ideas? and so forth. Pairing words and text effectively takes a great deal of critical skills. Teachers may want to use a few warm-up activities before students

Research

Critical Thinking

Process

Process

start working with storyboards. (See Appendix B: "Activity: Writing Words for Images" and "Activity: Evaluating Media Messages.")

Teachers may also want to model creating a storyboard using Microsoft Office PowerPoint, with each slide representing a box on the storyboard. As the teacher and students construct particular frames, the teacher can remind students about the characteristics of a good visual nonfiction essay, such as narrow focus, well suited to a visual medium, and audience appeal, which they discussed as a class back when students were getting ready to select their topics. These criteria will help inform the decisions the students will need to make, especially with regard to print and image content and transitions.

Collaboration

As Chad, Connor, and Jerad sat down to create their storyboard, they made the decision that Chad would be the scribe of the storyboard, Jerad would use the computer to seek additional information, and Connor would consult the print sources, including the historical novel *The Sea of Trolls* (Farmer 2006), as needed. (Note: Students had the option to do a print-based storyboard first, which this group chose to do.) Follow frame by frame as the plan for their visual nonfiction essay evolves:

Figure 7.1 *Storyboard Frame*

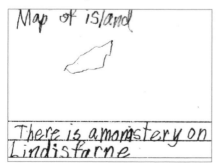

**Chad:** Maybe we should have an introduction and then the title.
**Connor:** Like *793.*
**Chad:** Like *793.* Is that right?
**Connor:** I'm looking. It's right here [in the appendix]. *793. June 8, 793.*

**Connor:** Maybe the first slide should be just *793 Dot, dot, dot.* Or *June 8, 793, dot, dot dot.* So what happens next?
**Chad:** But it has to be A.D.

Figure 7.2 *Storyboard Frame 2*

**Chad:** A monastery on Lindisfarne. Okay, wait. On Lindisfarne. There is a peaceful monastery. Does that sound cool? Do you want to do a voice-over?
**Connor:** No.
**Chad:** Nah. On second thought, that would kind of take away from it.
**Connor:** Maybe we could have some music right there.
**Chad:** [Writing.] On the island Lindisfarne, there is a monastery living peacefully.

**Jerad:** Then we could maybe have a picture. Like a big house or something like that.
**Connor:** Or a map.

Figure 7.3 *Storyboard Frame 3*

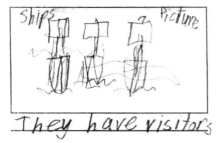

**Jerad:** Then the monks rushed to the shores to meet their unexpected visitors.
**Chad:** No, they have visitors.
**Jerad:** Then have a picture of ships.
**Chad:** Yeah, ships.
**Chad:** [Drawing ships.] Don't make fun of my drawing. I know it's not perfect.
**Jerad:** I'm not making fun; it's a small sketch. It looks good. It will help us know what to look for.

Figure 7.4 *Storyboard Frame 4*

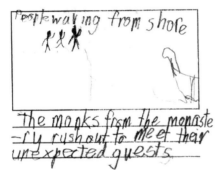

**Chad:** So, Connor, they rush out to meet them. The monks rushed out. Should we say the monks from the monastery?
**Jerad:** The monks rushed out to meet their unexpected visitors.
**Connor:** What pictures should we have in here? We want something dramatic like people going out to the shore. People waving.

Figure 7.5 *Storyboard Frame 5*

**Chad:** Also a picture of a Viking with an ax coming from the ship or something.
**Jerad:** On its own page, we should say that the Vikings are not who [the monks] think they are.
**Chad:** But they came out to meet their unexpected guests. Or say these guests had sinister intentions.

**Jerad:** Should we put *The Destruction of Lindisfarne* or *The Raiding of Lindisfarne*?
**Connor:** They didn't destroy Lindisfarne. Put *The Destruction of the Holy Isle* because that is what they destroyed. Say *Destruction* because it was an attack.
**Chad:** Yeah, [the Vikings] became the terror of the world as they attacked an innocent monastery.

Figure 7.6 *Storyboard Frame 6*

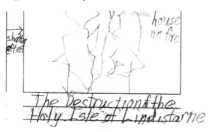

**Connor:** Now show a house burning, because, remember, they set it on fire.
**Jerad:** So we could just say the title on that slide, *The Destruction of the Holy Isle of Lindisfarne*?
**Chad:** That's fine.

Figure 7.7 *Storyboard Frame 7*

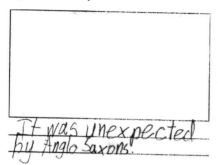

**Jerad:** [Looking at a source.] It says, "it was completely unexpected."

**Chad:** We can't say that because that's exactly what the book says. We have to reword it or it's plagiarism.

**Jerad:** Say, "It took the Saxons completely by surprise because no one thought they would attack a monastery."

**Chad:** Keep it simple. We can't have a lot of text on each slide. Put *The Anglo Saxons did not expect the attack*.

**Jerad:** I'm going to put *It was unexpected by Anglo Saxons*.

[The boys are looking in a book for an image for the slide.]

**Chad:** Actually, we could not put an image here. Just the text. It will make it more dramatic-y.

Figure 7.8 *Storyboard Frame 8*

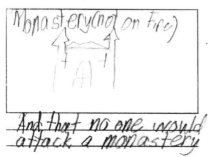

**Chad:** Then we could say that the sea protected them, except from the Vikings.

**Jerad:** They believed the sea protected them. That sounds better.

[The boys are looking in a book for an image for the slide.]

**Chad:** Who's going to take this seriously? We're not finding what we need. We're going to have to take a vacation to where the Vikings started out and take lots of pictures while we're there.

**Jerad:** Just tell them you are a bard.

**Connor:** We can take a picture from this book. Look.

**Chad:** Oh, yeah. That's perfect.

**Jerad:** We can change this later. Let's just keep going to see where this is going. We're probably going to have to shorten this later.

Figure 7.9 *Storyboard Frame 9*

**Chad:** Alright, listen. No one thought anyone would attack the monastery, except the Vikings proved them wrong. Or, like, but the Vikings would.

**Jerad:** Yeah, put that.

**Chad:** Do you want to call them Vikings or Northmen?

**Jerad:** Northmen.

**Connor:** Do you want this picture of the burning house?

**Jerad:** Yes.

Figure 7.10 *Storyboard Frame 10*

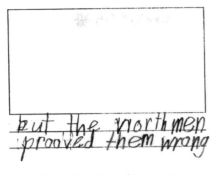

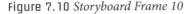

Figure 7.11 *Storyboard Frame 11*

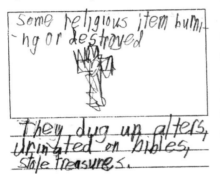

**Jerad:** Put that, but put it on another slide. Put *They proved them wrong* on this slide.

**Chad:** Yeah, that's good. It's more dramatic.

**Connor:** [Reading from a source.] It says, "They slayed the nuns. They took the rest captive. They climbed into the ships and sailed away. The attacks shocked the people of Europe. . . ."

**Chad:** So that's great. Let's go into the various ways they were killed. I did research on that part. . . .

**Chad:** Connor, what do you want me to put after this?

**Connor:** That the Northmen proved them wrong.

**Chad:** We have that. Look. I did that while you were reading.

**Jerad:** [Laughing.] The pillagers pillaged.

**Chad:** [Laughing.] They pillaged the village.

**Connor:** We can find an image for that. Something religious and then we can put flames around it. Put a note there that we're going to find that.

**Chad:** Okay. I'm going to write a few things they did. They stole treasures. They urinated on the bibles.

**Jerad:** Yes, strongly word that. Because they destroyed the altars. We have to tell what they did.

Figure 7.12 *Storyboard Frame 12*

**Connor:** Separate what they did to the things, and what they did to the people.

**Chad:** We can make it dramatic. Put it on different slides.

Figure 7.13 *Storyboard Frame 13*

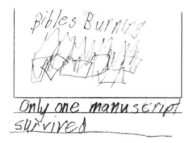

**Connor:** They took some away in fetters.

**Jerad:** What are fetters?

**Chad:** Like chains. Cages, I think. I read about that. Let me find it.

**Jerad:** Does fetters need to be capitalized?

**Connor:** No. Look. Read this part right here.

**Chad:** Others they drowned and some they drowned later at sea.

Figure 7.14 *Storyboard Frame 14*

**Chad:** It's too much on one slide.

**Connor:** Put the drowning part in another slide.

**Jerad:** Yeah, we can have an image of them at sea.

**Connor:** Okay. Yes, draw that. Just put a note. We're almost out of time. Let's keep going.

Figure 7.15 *Storyboard Frame 15*

**Jerad:** And then there was one manuscript that survived.

**Connor:** But let's put lots of things that didn't make it to make everyone wonder what it is.

**Chad:** Yeah, be dramatic. Because we're not doing a voice-over, but we can still be dramatic. By putting it on its own slide.

**Connor:** So what is the text?

**Jerad:** Only one manuscript survived.

Figure 7.16 *Storyboard Frame 16*

**Chad:** Next slide is just *The Lindisfarne Bible.* Connor, you have a picture of that already, right?

**Connor:** Yes. Okay. Let's go back because here are some other Viking pictures. And here is another ship; it is sailing.

**Jerad:** Those are good. Make a note of that.

Figure 7.17 *Storyboard Frame 17*

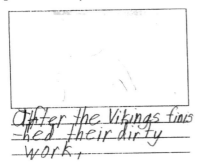

**Jerad:** Now are we doing the credits?

**Chad:** No. Let's end it. Write *Once the Vikings finished doing their dirty work.*

**Connor:** Okay. Do we have too much? Forty slides at ten seconds that would be five minutes.

**Chad:** That would be the most incredibly boring thing ever done.

**Connor:** Okay. We have to put that they left.

**Jerad:** Yeah. Like he said, "After the Vikings finished their dirty work." Got it.

Figure 7.18 *Storyboard Frame 18*

**Jerad:** Right. They returned to their ship. [Chad writes.]

**Jerad:** It has to be two minutes, remember?

**Connor:** We can upload a picture for this. Draw a Viking ship there.

Figure 7.19 *Storyboard Frame 19*

**Connor:** Put *and left* there. *And left!* [Chad writes.]

**Jerad:** Put *Only one thing could survive such a massive attack.*

**Chad:** Yeah, but I don't think we should put that. We have to stick to the facts.

Figure 7.20 *Storyboard Frame 20*

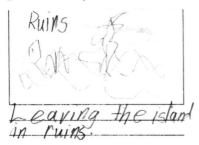

**Jerad:** The Vikings would become a curse.

**Connor:** Through certain parts of Europe. This attack would leave the rest of Europe . . .

**Chad:** We can't put that unless we can find that in our sources.

**Chad:** Connor, will you get a picture of an island? You want to end it with this?

Figure 7.21 *Storyboard Frame 21*

Credits

**Jerad:** Yes. We then put the credits.

**Connor:** We've got to add the pictures. We've got these websites. Pictures from [free image website]. I'll use the pictures on the storyboard to know what I've got to get from the Internet.

As students were in the act of creating the storyboard, they toggled between words and images, and their messages were defined and refined by their ability to select and deselect, adjust and readjust, based on what they could find or not find in their research. They used the storyboard to engage in conversation that allowed them to take stock of their research and devise a plan for presenting it as a visual nonfiction essay.

# Putting the Essay Together

Having constructed storyboards, students now have a plan for putting their research together as a visual nonfiction essay. Those students who worked on paper during storyboarding will need to create PowerPoint slides of the words and images they planned. Those students who created their storyboards in PowerPoint can begin importing their slides to Movie Maker. Teachers will likely need to provide some instruction or review about this process and can do so by showing a how-to video easily accessed from YouTube and/or by asking students who have experience with Movie Maker to help those students who are new to the software.

Using technology to transform print into a visual form requires that students make many more decisions about effective, and often creative, approaches for delivering the content. For instance, as the students participating in this project began working from their storyboards, they thought about the visual nonfiction essay as a whole and contemplated many of these questions:

- Will our main message be clear?
- Is the information concise?
- How do the main ideas fit together?
- What is the mood we want to create?
- How can text, images, and music be used to create the mood?
- What special effects do we have available?

Then as students constructed each slide of the visual nonfiction essay, transitioning from static image in PowerPoint to moving image in Movie Maker, they had to think critically about how each slide could contribute effectively to the visual nonfiction essay as a whole. They addressed many of these questions:

- Do we want to use text or voice-over?
- How can we transition from this idea to the next idea?
- What image(s) should we use?
- Is the image(s) authentic to the time period?
- What mood is created by the image(s)?
- How does the image(s) fit with the text?
- Can music be used to create a mood?
- How should the text and image(s) be placed on the slide?
- What other tools can be used to enhance the visual effect?

Clearly, presenting research as a visual nonfiction essay aided by technology provides students with more options as writers and producers of a text than is possible with paper and pen alone. Technology as a writing tool changes how students view the writing process. In this section, we discuss some of the benefits students realized as a result of creating a visual nonfiction essay. (See Figure 7.22 beforehand to learn about the students' final products.)

Figure 7.22 [part 1] *Descriptions of Students' Visual Nonfiction Essays*

1. "The Destruction of the Holy Island" (inspired by *The Sea of Trolls* [Farmer 2006])

   This visual nonfiction essay begins ominously with a black screen along with chanting and the heavy beating of drums. The opening text informs viewers that in 793, an island named Lindisfarne was home to monks who lived peacefully. Then, signaling a shift, the word *But* appears alone on the screen. Viewers learn, heartbreakingly, that the monks rushed out to greet their visitors because they had no idea that the visitors "had sinister intentions." What follows are a number of details, presented with both text and graphics, of the Saxons' destruction of the island—they "burnt crosses," "turned over alters," "urinated on bibles"—and the treatment of the island people—they were "killed," "taken in fetters," "drowned in the sea." The depressed mood of the essay is enhanced because the words appear first on a black screen and then images—of fire, burning crosses, and a handprint set aflame—slowly come into view behind the words. As the music quickens, viewers discover that only one artifact survived—the Lindisfarne Bible. The credits roll, identifying the title, authors, image sources, text sources, and music sources.

Figure 7.22 [part 2] *Descriptions of Students' Visual Nonfiction Essays*

2. "The Black Plague" (inspired by *I Am Rembrandt's Daughter* [Cullen 2007])
   This visual nonfiction essay begins by displaying the book cover of *I Am Rembrandt's Daughter*. Through voice-over, the narrator establishes the connection between the main characters of the book and the topic of the essay—the bubonic plague. Then information about the black plague is presented, including the cause (with an image of bacteria under a microscope), the scientist who identified it (with an image of his face that is part of a monument to him), and the people who suffered from it (with images of paintings from the time period showing the "buboes" that formed beneath the skin). The efforts people took to prevent and treat the symptoms are also described. Viewers may cringe to learn that cats and dogs, believed to be carriers of the disease, were killed, and leeches and burning hot metal were applied to affected areas of the body as treatments. The essay concludes with a map of Europe showing the afflicted areas in order to emphasize that the plague was widespread; the narrator adds the sobering fact that the plague killed around two million people. Enhanced by music, the rolling credits identify the authors and the print, electronic, and music sources.

3. "St. Patrick" (inspired by *Hush: An Irish Princess Tale* [Napoli 2007])
   With upbeat Irish music and images of clovers and Ireland's countryside, this visual nonfiction essay begins with an invitation from the narrator, through a voice-over, to viewers: "Welcome to the world of St. Patrick." The cheerful music fades deep into the background, however, as viewers learn early biographical information about St. Patrick: He was "captured by pirates," "lived a hard life as a slave," and "exposed to the frigid cold." The mood shifts and the volume of the music increases when viewers are told that St. Patrick successfully escaped at the age of 21 and over the course of many years, studied, taught, and became an influential religious leader. Included is the (short) story behind why St. Patrick is credited with influencing Ireland to name the shamrock as the national flower. The essay, having presented more than twenty images as well as the significant events and influence of St. Patrick's life, concludes with the narrator commenting, "St. Patrick will always be remembered as a wave of good hope." More spirited Irish music plays as the credits roll. Viewers who pay attention will catch the authors' tongue-in-cheek display of "sources" followed by "more sources."

**Figure 7.22 (part 3)** *Descriptions of Students' Visual Nonfiction Essays*

4.  "Saladin" (inspired by *Blood Red Horse* [Grant 2004])
    This visual nonfiction essay begins with an image of a painting of Saladin. From voice-over narration, viewers learn biographical information about Saladin, including that he was orphaned after a Crusader raid but overcame odds to become a great sultan of Egypt and Syria, beginning a new Muslim dynasty. Then Saladin's unique strategies for battling against the Crusaders are explained: "He poisoned his own city's wells so that if the Crusaders captured them, the city would be of no use," and "he had special soldiers who worked with a form of Greek fire, which stuck to everything and terrified the Christians." Viewers learn that Saladin's strategies caused King Richard to enact a peace treaty with Saladin, "the greatest Muslim leader of all time." Images of depictions of the Crusades and a map titled *Dominions of Saladin* are used to underscore the essay's main points. Music plays as the credits roll, specifying websites, books, and music that supported the essay.

5.  "Rembrandt" (inspired by *I Am Rembrandt's Daughter* [Cullen 2007])
    This visual nonfiction essay focuses on Rembrandt's later life and describes a change in his artistic style and the consequences of that choice. Music plays in the background throughout the essay, and the authors choose to alternate between text and image to make their points rather than depend on voice-over narration. When examining Rembrandt's artistic style, the authors use Microsoft AutoShapes to point out how some colors stand out against others; doing so helps viewers understand the concept that Rembrandt contrasted light and dark in his paintings. Throughout the essay, a dozen of Rembrandt's paintings and etchings are featured for the viewers' enjoyment. Closing credits identify the authors' print, online, and music sources.

6.  "Leonardo da Vinci" (inspired by *The Second Mrs. Gioconda* [Konigsburg 1975])
    This visual nonfiction essay features a special voice-over narrator: Mona Lisa herself! In an awkwardly squeaky voice, complete with a rough Italian accent, Mona Lisa guides viewers through a description of the Renaissance period (for example, "people rethought classical ways and theories" and "science flourished") and the masterpieces of her "friend," artist Leonardo da Vinci.

Figure 7.22 (part 4) *Descriptions of Students' Visual Nonfiction Essays*

To highlight their main points, the authors use images of several of Leonardo's paintings, add speech bubbles, and incorporate slides with multiple images, colors, and other features and effects. The authors also inserted humorous quips (for example, "Mama Mia!" is shouted after especially amazing facts about Leonardo), and many captions are intentionally playful (for example, "*The Virgin of the Rocks* Rocks"). The essay ends with the narcissistic narrator's review of the painting of herself, complimenting the artist on his ability to create "heavenly, gothic-like qualities" and "a mystery behind the smile." In the credits, viewers learn the real identify of the narrator, along with the authors of the essay and the sources they consulted.

7. "Knights and Their Horses" (inspired by *Blood Red Horse* [Grant 2004])
This visual nonfiction essay begins with the thesis that knights were a crucial resource for winning battles for the Christians. What follows is a comprehensive overview of the ways in which knights protected themselves from head to toe. Voice-over narration provides several sentences of researched information about the purpose and use of each weapon while an image of that weapon is displayed. The role of the knights' horses and the armor used to protect the horses are also explained. Music and the crediting of sources complete the essay.

# Benefits of Creating a Visual Nonfiction Essay

Why construct a visual nonfiction essay? Here are five ways in which students honed their literacy and technology skills.

## 1. Students researched and analyzed throughout the process.

Research is not a fixed step in the process; it undergirds all stages of the process. Throughout each stage—reading, creating independent projects, and storyboarding—the need for research often emerges naturally.

Sometimes students had to return to research to verify information they wanted to include in their visual nonfiction essay:

**Melissa:** Do you want to say this?

**Jessica:** What?

**Melissa:** That Rembrandt made more than one hundred paintings.

**Jessica:** Yes.

**Melissa:** Okay. Including forty-one etchings and thirty-seven self-portraits?

**Jessica:** Etchings are not paintings. I thought I saw that it said he drew seventy paintings and forty-one etchings.

**Melissa:** Let's check that.

In most cases, students' initial research yielded a great deal of information that informed the content of the visual nonfiction essay, but when it was time to add images to support their points, they had to return to their sources. While one of the groups working from *I Am Rembrandt's Daughter* had conducted a lot of information about Rembrandt's later life and the change in his technique that made Rembrandt fall out of favor, when it was time to add images to the essay, they needed to be able to identify and learn more about Rembrandt's paintings. For example, group member Melissa commented:

> We want people to know about how he painted. How he was different and what made him popular and then not popular. But we are still working on finding some information. We are finding more information for some of these paintings we're putting in. We are also trying to find a self-portrait.

The initial phase of research provided students with dependable sources that they could return to again and again. As students worked to present their information in a visual form, they continually asked themselves, "What do we have?" and "What do we need?" As a result, the research process was seamless, recurrent, and natural.

### 2. Students toggled between content and image to make decisions about their message.

A written research essay essentially requires students to present in words a synthesis of their research. A visual nonfiction essay, though, complicates matters by asking students to meld words and images. As a result, students toggle between content and image as they construct visual nonfiction essays.

The visual nonfiction essay required students to interpret their content visually and to convey that print and visual content in a way that would make sense to their audience, the viewers. That task required students to think deeply about the features, qualities, and messages of images; a group working from *The Sea of Trolls* did just that when they debated which of a few images best matched their content:

Audience

**Connor:** I think this one will work better for [representing] "The Vikings came with sinister intentions," and it is clearer than that [image].

**Jerad:** Why is that one better?

**Connor:** Because it is more, like, it has more tension.

**Chad:** And it's hard to see that picture [the original one they used].

**Connor:** Should I put it in?

**Chad:** Yes. This kind of explains the irony. That most have lived here for many years peacefully. Put it right before that slide. It transitions to the part about sinister intentions. It's like you're introducing the next picture, which is going to be scary!

**Jerad:** Make it dark. Black.

Sometimes groups discovered that although they found images to coalesce with content perfectly, they wondered how they could help the viewer see the connection. For instance, Jessica and Melissa, whose visual nonfiction essay covered the later life and paintings of Rembrandt, wanted to ensure that viewers would understand one of Rembrandt's painting styles, a point that was central to the message of the visual nonfiction essay as a whole. One student knew a technological tool that could help. (See Figure 7.23.)

Figure 7.23 *Using Microsoft AutoScript  to Clarify a Point*

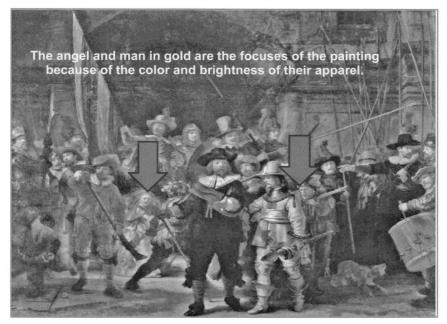

**Jessica:** We should have one of his most famous paintings to show light and dark.

**Melissa:** Show it and then say that it shows the contrast of light and dark.

**Jessica:** We have to point it out. We could have the picture right here and have arrows popping up saying this.

**Melissa:** How?

**Jessica:** With Microsoft [Auto]Shapes.

**Melissa:** Hold on. Show me.

**Jessica:** We will point to their faces to show light and point to the background to show dark.

In another instance, students discussed how to end their essay. One student suggested that they could tell when and how Rembrandt died; the other student, however, thought about the message of the essay and suggested that a final slide could contain both print and image in order to convey the message of the essay—that Rembrandt is remembered still today:

**Melissa:** So how do we conclude?

**Jessica:** Maybe we could do how he died and when.

**Melissa:** Yes, and then we could add another slide and say this is one of his most famous pictures?

**Jessica:** How he died and when? How many slides do we have?

**Melissa:** [Regardless] I think we have to have a conclusion to say how he died and that he is remembered.

Collaboration

In these cases and many more, constructing a visual nonfiction essay created a dynamic that is absent from writing a print-only essay. Adding images to convey content and weighing how the content and images may be interpreted by viewers enhanced the experience of producing a visual nonfiction essay.

### 3. Students considered many features when creating a visual text.

Students' initial research efforts focused on finding good content to present, but when students transitioned to determining how to present that content in visual form, they were confronted with many more considerations. Specifically, students had to think about the ways in which length, format, voice-overs, transitions, color and background, and other effects could enhance or detract from their visual nonfiction essays.

Genre
Learning

As students were researching and storyboarding, they planned the content they felt they could feasibly present in the essay. And while producing the visual nonfiction essay, discussions continued about ways to economize the material they wanted to include. After covering just one of their main points, Jessica and Melissa realized space was at a premium:

**Jessica:** Let's keep going. How long do you think the essay is so far?

**Melissa:** Well, right now, it is six slides. Probably about five or so seconds each. So like forty-two seconds so far. We've got to move on because we want to talk about his wife, his painting style, where he lived . . . .

Sometimes having to make cuts to content was painful:

**Patrick:** But I think that is neat.

**Adrian:** We just don't have the space.

Other times, the time restriction helped students remain focused on what mattered in terms of topic coverage:

**Sergio:** We have to put in information about Arabic.

**Adrian:** Patrick, you're looking at tactics, right?

**Keith:** Listen, we're going to tell the story of how Saladin used tactics and destroyed the Crusaders. That is basically all we have time to do.

In this short exchange, Keith reminded the group that not all ideas were related enough to their central focus to be used.

The nature of the visual nonfiction essay is that these students had virtually limitless choices in terms of presentation style. Formatting matters had to be debated by the groups; for example, one group wanted to incorporate voice-over in order to give the essay cohesion:

**Sergio:** We can do the voice-over and then see how long we talk [and maybe cut it in some places].

**Adrian:** We don't want to make it different in every single [slide]; it would be kind of distracting [otherwise].

This group later discussed that the use of voice-over allowed them to "make transitions" from one main topic to another. But another group thought that voice-over narration would actually detract from the message:

**Chad:** Do you want to do a voice-over?

**Jerad:** No, well, maybe at the beginning. . . . On second thought, that might take away the effect.

Format considerations often gave way to considering how to dole out the content. As students worked from their storyboards to create their essays, they often realized that they had planned too much content and text for particular slides. They discussed that the power and effect of the essay would be increased if they gave viewers smaller bits of information to digest. Here is one group's discussion of strengthening the punch of a main idea:

> **Arial:** I was thinking, Why don't we do one line [on this slide] and one line [on the next slide]?
> **Emelia** [working on the computer]: Like this? Separate the ideas?
> **Arial:** Yes. Make them two ideas. But do you like the old way?
> **Emelia:** No. It's better [your way].

Revision

Another group, working on an essay about the destruction of the Holy Isle, deviated from their storyboard in a number of instances. Because they found more images than they thought they might, they decided to stretch out their content and, as one student commented, "make the whole thing more intense."

Audience

Presenting information visually made students consider the artistic appeal of their essay. Often students experimented with the technological tools available to them until they were satisfied with the effects:

> **Keith:** Should I use this color or that color?
> **Adrian:** We need another color to go with it.
> **Keith:** That looks awesome.
> **Adrian:** Do you want this one?
> **Keith:** That one. It will go with the words.

Their conversations often centered around making the essay cohesive both within slides and across slides.

## 4. Students considered the accuracy and authenticity of their information, images, and music.

Unlike a research essay that deals in words, a visual nonfiction essay has many parts—information, images, music—that must fit together harmoniously, and any part that is inaccurate or inauthentic can stand out to the viewer, negatively impacting the overall effect. When putting together the visual nonfiction essay, students were often sent back to poke into their original sources or went in search of new sources in order to address matters of accuracy and authenticity.

One of the advantages of having several groups work on related topics was that they could share information. For two particular groups constructing visual nonfiction essays about the Crusades, authenticity was a critical matter:

**Group 1:** We are trying to find different horses, but it is not really working. We are looking for Arab horses, not European horses. We're stuck.

**Group 2:** We found a horse encyclopedia that is pretty awesome.

**Group 1:** We have to compare the tactics and horses during the Crusades. Is there an *Eyewitness* book on these things?

**Group 2:** Look here. The Arabian cutting horse.

**Group 1:** Perfect. I need something to write all this down. [Looks elsewhere in the encyclopedia.] We can't use this. It's stuff on a mythical horse captured at Cypress. Or the wild west.

Authenticity was a matter that applied not only to images but music as well. One group was frustrated, stating, "We really couldn't find that many pieces of music that fit our topic, and we wanted audio on our video." But with a little digging around on free music sites, they eventually found some clips that suited their essay:

*Genre Learning*

**Jerad:** Maybe we could use that song and then use the dramatic thing.

**Chad:** I like the Kyrie song [*Kyrie Christie Eleison*, a Gregorian chant]. It is very old.

**Jerad:** I think this is the Gregorian chant.

**Teacher:** Wasn't it primarily a monastery [that was attacked]? So that might actually work.

**Chad [to the teacher]:** Listen to the Kyrie one.

Beyond matching music to the time period, students had to consider whether the music they selected would enhance the mood of their essay:

*Audience*

**Chad:** That is too fast.

**Connor:** That is actually one of the Gregorian chants.

**Chad:** I know. But you are going to make a lot of people laugh if you use that.

**Connor:** Okay, here is one. This is more like it, right?

**Chad:** Yes! That is the one I wanted to use [earlier].

Throughout the process of selecting appropriate effects for the visual nonfiction essay, the students' research that yielded the content of their essay also played an important role in helping them make decisions about the images and music that would be appropriate to incorporate. Putting together the visual nonfiction essay made students keenly aware that all aspects had to work in concert.

### 5. *Students blended the writing process fluidly.*

In a visual nonfiction essay, as students think about how ideas fit together and how they could transition from one idea to the next, they also have to think about how visual images and technological tools can be used to clarify and extend their main ideas. Students engaged in discussions—both significant and multiple—in order to plan well:

Research

> **Emelia:** Which [storyboard box] should we open with?
> **Arial:** My favorite is definitely the merchant.
> **Emelia:** I don't like that one. We could use it, though.
> **Arial:** What is wrong with that one?
> **Emelia:** I think we need to talk about the anatomy lessons. Look, this [book] is very important [to the topic].

This difference of opinion sent the students back to their sources to muster support for their vision for how the visual nonfiction essay should begin.

Revision

As students worked from their storyboards to draft their essays, they were often revising as well. For example, Melissa and Jessica had planned out the text of their visual nonfiction essay on Rembrandt in great detail, but they had paid less attention to the images that they would use to match the text. Thus, the visual component of the essay required them to do some juggling while in the drafting phase:

> **Melissa:** Help me figure out what to say on the next slide, which is going to be black and white with arrows. Should we say, "Notice how the faces here are brighter than here"?
> **Jessica:** Are we using *The Night Watch*?
> **Melissa:** I thought we were going to use *The Night Watch* for another one.
> **Jessica:** Okay. Let's save it. Let's use this one. See how they have bright faces and clothes.
> **Melissa:** That's good.
> **Jessica:** We may need to come back and add one more. Make it black and type in something about how Rembrandt paints the faces brightly against the black clothing of the members of the guild.

Yet, students also knew moving too quickly toward revision could hamper the drafting stage. So, students often made plans for revision while staying within the drafting mode. In the previous excerpt, Jessica said, "We may need to come back and add one more." Revision also occurred often because students had multiple times to review their work. That is, students originally created PowerPoint slides and then took those slides and dropped them into Movie Maker. Working in Movie Maker, students could add all kinds of effects, such as images, music, voice-over narration, backgrounds and color, and so forth. As a specific example, voice-over narration allowed students to record a segment and play it back; hearing the content repeated back to them often helped them debate any flaws, refine the text, and then rerecord. Because Movie Maker allowed their visual nonfiction essays to be a series of moving images, students could "rewind" their essays as they constructed them and adjust, refine, and revise the content and effects until they were satisfied. They literally had myriad opportunities to "re-vision" their essay as they constructed it.

■ ▪ ■ ▪ ■ ▫

Authoring the visual nonfiction essay affords students the opportunity to engage with content about the time periods being researched, hone their technology skills, work collaboratively with peers, and become active decision makers as they co-construct well-researched texts. Driving the project is the anticipation of showcasing the topics the students self-select in a creative, perhaps humorous, perhaps dramatic, visually appealing way. The final products should clearly reveal how technology enhances the research process—multiple sources enable in-depth coverage of the topics, images enhance the written word, and special effects help the authors focus the viewers' attention on important ideas. Students also have the potential to acquire many important writing habits—establishing a manageable focus, organizing information, attending to conciseness and precision of expression, and synthesizing a large body of information. These writing habits will serve students well in future writing endeavors.

Empowerment

# Conclusion

Although "Reading and Writing to Launch Moviemaking" and "Authoring the Visual Nonfiction Essay" are very different, these two projects share many commonalities. At their core is an integration of multiple kinds of technology into more traditional reading and writing practices already common in literacy classrooms today. What shines through is that students who feel empowered have the potential to shape their own learning in boundless ways.

As we've explored throughout *When Writing with Technology Matters*, the projects are easy to follow and flexible enough to adjust to different grade levels of students or different topics of study; however, we know that you will want to design new projects—such as biographies, documentaries, and persuasive arguments about peer, school, and community issues—that will make writing with technology matter for *your* students. We end with a handful of key points for you to keep in mind as you implement your own projects.

• *Students need to be writing more.* With open-ended, multistep projects, students can produce a lot of writing. Teachers can (perhaps sneakily) engage students in numerous *forms* of writing, such as fiction writing, storyboarding, scriptwriting, pitches, job applications, nonfiction writing, research writing; many *genres* of writing, such as poetry, parodies, cartoons, and editorials; and in various *arrangements*, such as writing alone, writing together, writing on paper, and writing online. Writing every day or every few days on a blog, for instance, keeps students focused on their tasks as they report about their progress and indirectly fosters reflection on their learning. In addition, all of this writing serves as a formative assessment tool for teachers.

- *Students need sustained thinking time.* Probably too frequently the school day is divided into discrete chunks where learning is opened at the beginning of the class period and closed at the end of it. Technology has the potential to keep the learning going, so to speak. Writing on a blog and reading their peers' postings on a blog gets ideas percolating. Following research trails based on personal interests causes students to spend more time with texts and read more deeply. Projects that employ multistep processes that grow and shape a product organically provide opportunities for students to be thoughtful about their work. Thinking takes time.

- *Students need to write for real audiences.* Much of what students write is, unfortunately, for teachers and for grades. When students have an auditorium of family and friends or an anonymous audience of potentially thousands of viewers online, they feel they are writing for a real (and big) audience, which brings with it a more intense desire to create something good—captivating, even.

- *Students need to care about what they're writing.* Projects that involve multiple and integrated steps help students recognize that they have creative control to build toward something important. Technology makes information abundant and so readily accessible that literacy processes are less cumbersome and more sustainable. As tools become more versatile, learning becomes more individualized, and students tend to care more about what they produce and have a more positive and memorable experience.

- *Students need teachers to guide their learning.* Teachers will put in a lot of time designing projects that successfully integrate writing and technology while also sustaining students' motivation and engagement. That's a fact. But once students understand the essence of the project, teachers can then pull back and act as facilitators of students' experiences. Meaningful learning takes place when teachers provide the support that students need to willingly take risks.

Finally, the focus on twenty-first-century skills—collaboration, problem solving, decision making, critical thinking, and creativity—is a call to educators to reconsider what literacy work should look like. Collaboration should involve the desire to solve real problems by using complex decision making, which requires trial and error and extended periods of thinking time with people who are willing to challenge others' perspectives. Critical thinking is looking at a situation as having a range of possibilities as answers rather than one correct answer. When students are put together for extended periods of time and engage in the creative process, their learning is unpredictable and more dynamic than can likely be accomplished through more structured instructional practices and experiences.

Teachers who invest in these kinds of contexts in their literacy classrooms make writing with technology matter to students.

# Appendix A

## Contents

# Conducting a WebQuest

Using the links provided by your teacher, go on a quest for information on the book you have chosen to research:

1. Read the author's biography and note three interesting facts.

_____

_____

_____

2. Find a summary of the book.

_____

_____

_____

3. Determine the book's genre.

_____

4. Find something interesting or unusual to share about:
- something mentioned in a book review
- the themes explored by the author in the book
- whether the book has been adapted as a movie
- whether the book is part of a series
- whether the book is based on a true story
- what other books the author has written

_____

_____

_____

# Mini-Lesson: Poster of Possibilities

## Resource

Scieszka, J. 1989. *The True Story of the 3 Little Pigs!* New York: Puffin.

## Procedure

1. Read *The True Story of the 3 Little Pigs!* Have students compare this tale to the original version. Students will likely point out that in this tale, the wolf's perspective is that the pigs are at fault (the poorly built houses fell down) and therefore the wolf is not to blame for the pigs' demise.

2. Direct students' attention to the Poster of Possibilities (see Figure 3.1). Tell students that they will be selecting one or more of the options on the poster, which will guide how they will write the stories they wish to adapt into film.

3. Point to the third item on the list: "Tell the story from a different character's point of view." Discuss with students how *The True Story of the 3 Little Pigs!* is an example of this option.

4. Review the rest of the options, reading each one and defining unfamiliar terms (such as *sequel* or *prequel*). Divide the students into seven groups. Have each group draw one of the "possibilities cards" that follow.

5. Tell the groups to follow the instructions on their cards. (Decide if you want students to respond orally, to write short responses, to designate a note taker, and so forth.)

6. Allow each group to present its ideas. Reinforce the connection between the students' ideas and the movie poster options.

# Possibilities Cards

| | |
|---|---|
| **Move your characters to another setting.**<br><br>Select another setting; it could be a different time or a different place or both. How would this story of the wolf and pigs be different in another setting? | **Rewrite the story as if it happened in your world, with your friends and family.**<br><br>Think about the three pigs as your best friends and the school bully as the wolf. Now tell that story. |
| **Write the story with a visitor from another novel.**<br><br>Think about your favorite characters from other books (such as the wolf in *Little Red Riding Hood* or a goat from *Three Billy Goats Gruff*). Tell how the visiting character would change the story. | **Plan another outcome.**<br><br>To plan another outcome is to decide how the story would end differently. Tell what would have happened if one of the little pigs had given the wolf a cup of sugar. |
| **Write the sequel.**<br><br>Tell what would happen next if this story were to continue. | **Write the prequel.**<br><br>Tell the events that happened before this story began. |
| **Change a character's personality.**<br><br>Change the personality of the third little pig. Then tell how the story would be different as a result. | **Select your own possibility.** |

# Mini-Lesson: The Pitch

## Resource

Movie trailers found online

## Procedure

1. Screen movie trailer clips beforehand and select two clips that are appropriate to show to students. (We found many clips by simply Googling the words *movie trailers appropriate for children*. Students may enjoy the trailer for *Eragon* available at www.traileraddict.com.)

2. Define for students that a movie trailer is a short clip for the purpose of advertising a movie. Explain to students that they will be watching two movie trailers. Show the clips.

3. After viewing the clips, divide the students according to which trailer was their favorite. Set up a debate in which students discuss why they liked a particular clip. On the board, you might want to write these discussion starters:

   "I think the story will be about . . ."
   "I think I would like that movie because . . ."
   "I liked how the trailer showed that . . ."
   "I felt that this would be a better movie because . . ."
   "When I watched the clip, I felt . . ."

   As students share, record some of their ideas for all to see.

4. Distribute the handout and read through the section "Tips for Writing a Pitch." Ask students to review their recorded ideas to determine if their ideas correlated to any of the tips; discuss.

5. Distribute and read through the handout "A Model of a Pitch for *Gregor the Overlander*." Have students address how each of the tips was addressed in the model.

6. Students should now write a pitch for their own stories.

7. Allow students time to practice their delivery after reviewing the section "Tips for Delivering a Pitch."

# Tips for Writing and Delivering a Pitch

## *Tips for Writing a Pitch*

- Consider your audience.
  - Who are they? What are their interests? What would they want to see?
- Hook your listener.
  - How will you get your audience excited about this story? What makes your story worth seeing?
- Describe your story.
  - What is the story about? Who are the characters? What is the problem?
  - Keep it short (and don't give away the ending!).

## *Tips for Delivering a Pitch*

- Face your audience—don't turn your back on them!
- Keep eye contact with the audience.
- Speak clearly and loudly.
- Think about pacing. Speak faster to increase excitement and slower to add suspense.
- Be enthusiastic—you are selling your ideas.

# A Model of a Pitch for *Gregor the Overlander*

↓ Indicates movie is a sequel ↓
As Gregor yet again returns to the Underland,

↓ Establishes central character is on personal mission ↓
rescuing his father is the only thing on his mind.

↓ Identifies genre ↓     ↓ Tantalizes audience ↓
A hidden power is among him and it may

↓ Tantalizes audience ↓
cause great good or the destruction of all.

↓ Builds suspense ↓
Mareth and his friends think they know him. Think again!

# Tips for Conducting a Conference

### Read the story aloud.

- A conference partner reads the story aloud.
- The author of the story listens closely to see if the partner's expression matches how the author intends for the story to sound.
- The author should note when the reader stumbles. These areas might signal a conventions error or a problem with flow or logic.

### Prompts and questions for the author.

- Why did you write this story? (This helps the author think about the story's focus.)
- How did you want the audience to feel or react? (This helps the author think about the audience and mood.)
- Tell more about . . .
  - a certain character
  - a particular event (This helps the author consider if some ideas need clarification or elaboration.)
- Tell what you really like about your story. (This allows the author to share a favorite part and can be about the content or a writing technique.)

### Prompts and question for the author to ask the partner.

- What did you like about the story? (This allows the partner to react in a personal way.)
- What surprised you, scared you, made you smile or laugh, or made you sad? (This helps the author be aware of how the audience may react.)
- Was there something or someone you wanted to know more about? (This helps the author consider if some ideas need clarification or elaboration.)
- Tell me something you liked about the writing. (This allows the partner to point out a writing technique or interesting language.)

# Mini-Lesson: Storyboarding

## *Resource*

Stevens, J. 1995. *Tops and Bottoms*. New York: Houghton Mifflin Harcourt.

## *Procedure*

### *Part I: Understanding the Thinking Behind the Storyboard*

1.  Read the picture book *Tops and Bottoms*, or select and read another picture book with a strong story line.
2.  Hang a jump rope (or string) from one end of the chalkboard to another. Have clothespins nearby.
3.  Ask each student to draw a favorite scene from the book on an index card. Explain to the students that as a class, they will be using their drawings to retell the story in sequence.
4.  Have students gather around the rope. Ask a student to place his or her drawing in the center of the rope and tell about the scene.
5.  Then allow each student, one at a time, to place his or her drawing either before or after this first student's drawing. (If two students have drawn the same scene, place one drawing on top of the other.)
6.  After all the students have placed their drawings on the rope, ask the class whether it will be possible to tell the story using just the drawings. Lead a discussion to cover these points:
    > Are the essential plot events represented? (Add more drawings, if needed.)
    > Are there drawings that can be removed and the story will still make sense?
    > Why do you think some students drew the same event?
7.  After adjustments have been made to the drawings on the rope, begin reading the picture book again. Match the events of the text to the students' drawings, making sure that they are in the correct sequence. If needed, make adjustments.

### *Part II: Creating a Group Storyboard*

1.  Distribute the storyboard frame.
2.  Explain to students that the storyboard frame contains eight boxes that should be filled with drawings and text. Emphasize that the drawings and text should match and should sufficiently tell their group story in a correct sequence.

# Storyboard Frame

| | |
|---|---|
| | |
| | |
| | |
| | |

# Mini-Lesson: Comparing a Book to a Movie

*Resources*

Paterson, K. 1977. *Bridge to Terabithia*. New York: HarperCollins.

Csupo, G. 2007. *Bridge to Terabithia*. DVD recording. Walt Disney Pictures and Walden Media.

*Procedure*

1. Read the first two chapters of the book *Bridge to Terabithia*. (It is preferable that each student has a copy of the book because students will need to refer back to the text throughout the mini-lesson.) As they read, ask students to picture the text as a movie in their head.

2. Discuss the content and reread a few passages to point out the writer's craft as well as how characterization, setting, and plot are developed.

3. As a class, construct a storyboard of the events in the two chapters.

4. Watch the first seven minutes of the movie (stopping right after Leslie is introduced to the class and before the recess scene).

5. Now divide students into three groups and assign each group a category to discuss: character, setting, or plot. Distribute the "Guiding Questions" handout, which students can use to guide their discussions. Direct students to discuss the similarities and differences between the book and movie, and have them complete a Venn diagram. (See the "Answer Key" handout for examples.) Allow students to refer back to the book chapters, their storyboard, and the movie as needed.

6. As a class, have each of the three groups present their Venn diagrams. Using the "Answer Key" handout and other groups' ideas, add to each of the Venn diagrams.

# Guiding Questions for the Film *Bridge to Terabithia*

## *Characters and Their Relationships*

- What do we know about Jess and his family? (What are his interests? Where does he live? What are his responsibilities? What is his family like?)
- What do we know about Leslie and her family? (What are her interests? Where does she live? What are her responsibilities? What is her family like?)
- How is the dad portrayed in the book and in the movie? How do we know? (What is Dad's relationship with Jess?)

## *Setting*

- Where is the story taking place?
- When is the story taking place? (Time period: current day or long ago?) (What references do the author and moviemaker provide to help us know?)

## *Plot*

- What are the major events? (What is Jess doing/thinking/feeling? What is Leslie doing/thinking/feeling? How do they meet?)
- What are the conflicts?

# Answer Key for Guiding Questions for the Film *Bridge to Terabithia*

## Characters and Their Relationships

*What do we know about Jess and his family?*

What are his interests? Where does he live? What are his responsibilities? What is his family like?

**Book only:**

- Jess likes to draw. (Some students might wonder if the drawings at the beginning of the movie are Jess's and therefore think this is a similarity in the book and movie.)
- Jess's dad doesn't seem to like that Jess draws.
- Jess is responsible for milking the cows and picking beans.

**Both book and movie:**

- Jess seems closest to his sister May Belle, but is annoyed by her at times.
- Jess lives on a farm.
- Jess likes to run.
- Jess's family is poor.
- Jess has many sisters.

**Movie only:**

- Jess is responsible for taking care of the greenhouse.
- Jess is picked on by school kids.
- Jess's dad wanted him to have "boy shoes" and wished him luck in the race.

*What do we know about Leslie and her family?*

What are her interests? Where does she live? What are her responsibilities? What is her family like?

**Book only:**

- Leslie is Jess's new neighbor.
- Jess meets Leslie outside in the pasture near their homes.
- At first, Leslie's appearance makes Jess wonder if she is a tomboy.

*When Writing with Technology Matters* by Carol Bedard and Charles Fuhrken. Copyright © 2013. Stenhouse Publishers.

**Both book and movie:**

None.

**Movie only:**

- Leslie is a new girl at school.
- Jess meets Leslie in the classroom.
- Leslie has a lot of books in her book bag that she drops and spills.

## *How is Jess's dad portrayed? How do we know?*

What is Dad's relationship with Jess?

**Book only:**

- Jess wishes for a closer relationship with his dad, like he used to have (for example, wrestling with him on the floor).
- Jess's dad does not appreciate his drawings.

**Both book and movie:**

- Dad is portrayed as hardworking.

**Movie only:**

- Jess appears to have a close relationship with his dad (for example, Jess's dad asks Jess what is wrong and tries to convince the mother Jess needs new sneakers).

# Setting

*Where is the story taking place?*

**Book only:**

- On a farm only

**Both book and movie:**

- On a farm

**Movie only:**

- On a farm and in a classroom

## When is the story taking place? (Time period: current day or long ago?)

What references do the author and moviemaker provide to help us know?

**Book only:**

- Post-Vietnam era
    - Reference to teacher as "some kind of hippie."
    - Patriotic and folk song titles.

**Both book and movie:**

None.

**Movie only:**

- Modern day
    - Teacher tells students not to download reports.
    - Students shown wearing earphones.
    - Reference to free-lunch program.

## Plot

### What are the major events?

What is Jess doing/thinking/feeling? What is Leslie doing/thinking/feeling? How do they meet?

**Book only:**

- Jess won a race last year in school and works all summer because he wants to win again.
- Sisters go off shopping, but Jess has to stay behind to do chores.
- May Belle tells Jess that they have a new neighbor.
- Jess makes sandwiches, draws, and milks the cow.
- Jess meets Leslie the next morning.

**Both book and movie:**

- Jess runs in the morning.
- Sister complains at the breakfast table that he stinks after running.
- Jess has to do chores.

**Movie only:**

- Jess's mother throws away his old sneakers and gives him a hand-me-down pair.
- Kids call him "farmer boy" on the bus and tease him at school.
- Leslie is introduced to the class.

## *What are the conflicts?*

**Book only:**

- Jess wishes his relationship with his dad were different.
- Jess feels that he has a lot of responsibilities.
- Jess likes to draw but his drawings are not appreciated by his father or teachers.

**Both book and movie:**

- Jess is hassled by his sisters.

**Movie only:**

- Jess is teased by school kids about being a farm kid and about his shoes.
- Jess's teacher assumes he will act up in class as his sisters did.

# Mini-Lesson: Tools for Authors and Scriptwriters/Moviemakers

## *Resources*

Paterson, K. 1977. *Bridge to Terabithia*. New York: HarperCollins.

Csupo, G. (Director). 2007. *Bridge to Terabithia*. Walt Disney Pictures and Walden Media.

## *Procedure*

1.  Read the first two chapters of the book and review the first seven minutes of the movie.
2.  As a class, read and discuss the "Authors' Tools" handout that follows. Allow students to pair up to add additional examples. Share.
3.  Engage in a whole-class discussion about the following points:
    *   What is lost or gained when turning a text into a movie?
    *   What tools do authors and scriptwriters/moviemakers share and what tools are unique?
    *   What aha moments did you gain from this activity (such as realizing that movies do not follow the text word for word)?
4.  Using the "How Ideas Are Conveyed in *Bridge to Terabithia* (Book and Movie)" handout, discuss the first idea and examples.
5.  Have students complete the handout in small groups. Remind students to refer to their "Authors' Tools" and "Scriptwriters' and Moviemakers' Tools" handouts and encourage them to use a variety of tools.

# Authors' Tools

*Resource*

Paterson, K. 1977. *Bridge to Terabithia*. New York: HarperCollins.

| TOOL AND DEFINITION | EXAMPLE | ADD AN EXAMPLE |
|---|---|---|
| **Description**<br><br>The way that something is explained or told about. Authors strive for descriptive details that "show" rather than "tell." | "His breath was coming out in little puffs—cold for August." (page 2) | |
| **Narration**<br><br>A telling of the action (what is happening) in a particular sequence. | "Jess pushed his damp hair out of his face and plunked down on the wooden bench. He dumped two spoonfuls of sugar into his cup and slurped to keep the hot coffee from scalding his mouth." (page 5) | |
| **Dialogue**<br><br>A conversation between characters. Dialogue breaks up the narration and reveals what the characters are thinking. | "I hope they have a girl, six or seven," said May Belle. "I need somebody to play with."<br><br>"You got Joyce Ann."<br><br>"I hate Joyce Ann. She's nothing but a baby." (pages 9–10) | |

| | | |
|---|---|---|
| **Sensory and Figurative Language**<br><br>Sensory language appeals to the senses.<br><br>Figurative language (*such as similes, metaphors, personification, and hyperbole*) goes beyond a literal meaning. | "His straw-colored hair flapped hard against his forehead and his arms and legs flew out every which way." (page 3)<br><br>"He kept the knowledge of it inside him like a pirate treasure." (page 12) | |
| **Viewpoint/Perspective**<br><br>The position from which things are viewed and told. | "Sounds like some kind of hippie," his mother had said when Brenda, who had been in seventh grade last year, described Miss Edmunds to her.<br><br>She probably was. Jess wouldn't argue that, but he saw her as a beautiful wild creature who had been caught for a moment in that dirty old cage of a schoolhouse, perhaps by mistake. (pages 12–13) | |
| **Narrative Structure and Development**<br><br>A typical narrative structure contains exposition, rising action, climax, falling action, and resolution.<br><br>Development includes building a logical plot, round characters, tension, suspense, and so forth. | Building tension/conflict:<br><br>"Jess-*see*!"<br><br>Jess shoved the pad and pencils under his mattress and laid down flat, his heart thumping against the quilt. His mother was at the door. "You milk yet?"<br><br>He jumped off the bed. "Just going to." He dodged around her and out, grabbing the pail from beside the sink and the stool from beside the door, before she could ask him what he had been up to. (page 14) | |

*When Writing with Technology Matters* by Carol Bedard and Charles Fuhrken. Copyright © 2013. Stenhouse Publishers.

# Scriptwriters' and Moviemakers' Tools

*Resource*

Csupo, G. (Director). 2007. *Bridge to Terabithia*. Walt Disney Pictures and Walden Media.

| TOOL AND DEFINITION | EXAMPLE | ADD AN EXAMPLE |
|---|---|---|
| **Camera perspective/ movement/angles** <br><br> The craft of positioning and operating a camera to achieve a desired effect. | Long shot: View of farm (truck, house, and greenhouse) from a distance in opening scene. <br><br> Mid-shot: View of just Jess's legs while he is running. <br><br> Close-up shot: View of classroom teacher's mouth when lecturing the students about ground rules for the classroom. | |
| **Special effect** *(music/ sound/lighting/color)* <br><br> Visual or sound effects that set a tone and/or create a particular effect, such as tension. | While the credits are rolling at the beginning of the movie, Jess's drawings are interspersed with scenes of him running. | |
| **Dialogue** <br><br> A conversation between characters. Dialogue breaks up the action and reveals what the characters are thinking. | The kitchen scene with the parents talking in hushed tones about their finances. | |
| **Actors' expressions/ actions** <br><br> Conveying an idea or feeling through facial/ body movement. | Jess's facial expression— squinting and grimacing—after his older sister tells him, "You couldn't race in your old ones either." | |

| | | |
|---|---|---|
| **Set design/props/ costumes**<br><br>The physical surroundings and other elements that help viewers identify the context. | Authentic items related to the farmhouse (wood stacked on front porch) and the school (bus, chalkboard). | |
| **Narration** *(voice-over, flashback)*<br><br>Voice-over is "off-camera commentary" that shares what characters are thinking.<br><br>Flashback shares past events that help to understand present ones. | (No voice-over or flashback in the first seven minutes of the movie.) | |

# How Ideas Are Conveyed in
# *Bridge to Terabithia* (Book and Movie)

*Resources*

Paterson, K. 1977. *Bridge to Terabithia*. New York: HarperCollins.
Csupo, G. (Director). 2007. *Bridge to Terabithia*. Walt Disney Pictures and Walden Media.

| IDEA | BOOK | MOVIE |
|---|---|---|
| Jess's family is poor. | EXAMPLE:<br><br>Description: "The bottoms of his feet were by now as tough as his worn-out sneakers."<br><br>Dialogue: "Momma"—Brenda was starting again—"can't we have just one more [dollar]? So it'll be three [dollars] each?"<br><br>"No!" (page 7) | EXAMPLE:<br><br>Costume: Jess's running shoes are held together with tape.<br><br>Dialogue: "Consider it a free-lunch program, farmer boy." (Spoken by Janice, the bully.) |
| Jess is a runner. | | |
| Jess loves May Belle but is annoyed by her also. | | |

| | | |
|---|---|---|
| Jess is responsible. | | |
| Jess is a talented artist. | | |
| Jess's dad is hardworking. | | |

# Mini-Lesson: Turning a Story into a Script

*Procedure*

1.  Distribute the story and script sample that follows. Read together as a class.
2.  Help students understand the kinds of thinking they will need to do when they adapt their stories to scripts by discussing these questions:
    *   How is the first sentence of the story shown and elaborated in the script?
    *   How is the second sentence of the story shown and elaborated in the script?
    *   How is the third sentence of the story shown and elaborated in the script?
    *   What information in the script will help the actors playing the characters?
    *   What are other things to consider when writing a script?

# Story and Script Sample

---

### STORY

Back at school, Mrs. Lumer tasted almost everyone's snack, and decided that Anthony made the best. She didn't check Zeke's, which made him mad at Anthony. He wanted the money from his granola bar sales.

---

### SCRIPT

**INT – LUMER'S CLASS – DAY**
Lots of kids chatting and throwing spitballs.

    **MRS. LUMER:** Okay class, let's see what you made. Exceptional, Skipper . . .
        Mmm . . . C+. Martha . . . Nice.
Anthony tidies himself.

    **ANTHONY:** I hope you like it, Mrs. Lumer.

    **MRS. LUMER:** Anthony, this is just splendid! The most wonderful thing
        I've ever tasted! You are the winner of the contest!

    **ZEKE:** What about mine?

    **MRS. LUMER:** I doubt yours is better than Anthony's.
Zeke mumbles, clenches his fists tightly, rolls his eyes. He goes back to his desk and puts down his head.

    **ZEKE:** I've got to get his profits.

---

# Moviemaking Rubric

| | Exemplary (3) | Proficient (2) | Somewhat Proficient (1) | Unsatisfactory (0) |
|---|---|---|---|---|
| **Storyboard** | Storyboard contains relevant text, image, and filming information and shows evidence of thought and decision making. | Storyboard contains mostly relevant text, image, and filming information and shows some evidence of thought and decision making. | Storyboard contains some irrelevant text, image, and filming information and may show insufficient thought and decision making. | Storyboard contains text, image, and filming information that is irrelevant, vague, or altogether missing and shows little thought and decision making. |
| **Collaboration** | Group members utilized their individual strengths and managed time well. | Group members mostly worked well together to complete tasks on time. | Group members usually worked well together, but time and effort could have been planned better. | Group members did not work collaboratively and planned time poorly. |
| **Story** | The story has a clear beginning, middle, and end, and has well-developed characters and appropriate dialogue and action that enrich the story. | The story mostly feels complete and has developed characters and dialogue and action that contribute logically to the story. | The story feels somewhat incomplete, unoriginal, or predictable. Some characters, dialogue, and/or action might distract viewers. | The story is incomplete and confusing with characters, dialogue, and/or action that do not serve a purpose. |
| **Production** | Overall quality is very high. Special effects (such as slow motion or music) enhance the story. Transitions from scene to scene are smooth. | Overall quality is good. Special effects show thought and effort to contribute to the story. Transitions are generally well paced. | Overall quality has high and low points. Special effects are few and/or do not always make the story line better. Transitions are awkward at times. | Overall quality is low. Special effects are missing entirely or awkward and distracting. Transitions are often jarring. |
| **Overall Appeal** | The movie is entertaining and contains a few surprises that will likely impress viewers. | The movie is entertaining overall and contains some elements that viewers will likely enjoy. | The movie has some moments that viewers will likely find entertaining. | The movie has too many problems (artistic and/or technical) that take away from the entertainment value. |

# Mini-Lesson: Operating a Camera

## Resources
Several digital cameras
Television and connecting cables (optional)

## Procedure

1. Establish a few simple safety rules or procedures about using the camera, such as:
   - The camera must be firmly connected to the tripod (if one is being used).
   - The shoulder strap should be worn if the camera is being handheld.
   - Do not try to fix the camera yourself if you encounter a problem. Report the problem to the teacher.
   - Follow a check-out, check-in routine for issuing and collecting the cameras each day.
   - Charge batteries daily to avoid having to use cords and electric outlets and thereby creating safety hazards.
2. Help students become familiar with the parts of the camera (such as the on/off button, viewing window, and so on).
3. Distribute the handout "Basic Camera Techniques" that follows. Discuss and review the terms and the definitions.
4. Allow students to practice each of the types of shots by using the suggestions in the "Try It!" column. If desired, attach a camera to a television using the appropriate cables and model taking a particular kind of shot, allowing all students to view and learn from the demonstration.
5. If more practice is needed, allow students to come up with different scenarios and settings (such as outside) for filming.

# Basic Camera Techniques

| Term | Definition | Try It! |
|------|-----------|---------|
| **Close-up** | Shows the character close up; this shot reveals facial expressions and reactions. | Film one student's teeth. |
| **Mid-shot** | Shows the character from the waist up and their surroundings. | Film your teacher walking around the classroom. |
| **Long shot** | Shows the character and the surroundings from a distance. | Film one corner of your classroom by standing in the opposite corner. |
| **Low angle** | A shot taken from the ground level facing upward; the effect is to make the character stand out or look larger. | Lying on the ground, film your teacher writing on the board. |
| **High angle** | A shot taken from above the action; the effect is to make the character look smaller. | Standing on a sturdy surface, film a student who is sitting at a desk and writing. |
| **Panning** | Moving from side to side smoothly and slowly. | Standing in the front of the room, film the entire classroom from left to right. |
| **Zooming** | Moving the camera lens to make the character look closer or farther away. | Standing in the back of the room, first film a group of students and then narrow the shot until only one student is shown. |

# Mini-Lesson: Moviemaking Jobs

## *Resources*

Paterson, K. 1977. *Bridge to Terabithia*. New York: HarperCollins.
Csupo, G. (Director). 2007. *Bridge to Terabithia*. Walt Disney Pictures and Walden Media.

## *Procedure*

1.  Read the first two chapters of the book and review the first seven minutes of the movie. Allow students time to share similarities and differences between the book and movie.
2.  Distribute the handout "From Print to Screen" that follows.
3.  Review the guiding questions found on the handout.
4.  Replay the first seven minutes of the movie and have students complete the handout by recording their observations about the various jobs in moviemaking.
5.  Allow students to share what they noticed, such as:
    *   What do actors do? (set designers? directors? camera operators? editors?)
    *   What skills are needed to do these jobs?
    *   What jobs would you be good at and why?

# From Print to Screen

## *What do you notice about the . . .*

| Actors | Set Designers | Director | Camera Operators | Editors |
|---|---|---|---|---|
| | | | | |

Think about . . .

**Actors**
What do they say, do, and feel?
What do others say and think about them?

**Set Designers**
How is the setting established through set design?
What props and costuming are used?

**Director**
How did the director change the story or keep it the same?

**Camera Operators**
What camera positions/angles (close-up, mid-shot, long shot, low or high angle) are used?
What camera movements (panning, zooming, tracking, tilting) are used?

**Editors**
What special effects (music/sound effects, slow motion, narration) are added?

# Moviemaking Job Application

There are four positions available: **actor**, **set designer**, **director**, or **camera operator**. The positions are competitive, so complete the chart fully by writing about all of your skills and previous experiences.

| RANKING | JOB | QUALIFICATIONS |
|---|---|---|
| First choice | | |
| Second choice | | |
| Third choice | | |
| Fourth choice | | |

*When Writing with Technology Matters* by Carol Bedard and Charles Fuhrken. Copyright © 2013. Stenhouse Publishers.

# Appendix B

## Contents

# Conducting a WebQuest

Using the links provided by your teacher, go on a quest for information on the book you have chosen to research:

1. Read the author's biography and note three interesting facts.

_____

_____

_____

2. Find a summary of the book.

_____

_____

_____

3. Determine the book's time period.

_____

4. Find something interesting or unusual to share about:
   - something mentioned in a book review
   - whether the book is part of a series
   - what other books the author has written
   - the period in which the book is set
   - the form or style of the book (for example, told in letters, told in poems, and so on)

_____

_____

5. Explain the historical events that are the foundation of the book.

_____

_____

_When Writing with Technology Matters_ by Carol Bedard and Charles Fuhrken. Copyright © 2013. Stenhouse Publishers.

# Vocabulary and Historical References Log

As you read, look for interesting words, phrases, and historical events and/or people. Record them, the page number, and the meaning or significance.

| Words, Phrases, Historical Events and/or People | Page Number | Meaning/Significance |
|---|---|---|
|  |  |  |
|  |  |  |
|  |  |  |
|  |  |  |
|  |  |  |
|  |  |  |
|  |  |  |
|  |  |  |
|  |  |  |
|  |  |  |

# Credibility of Sources

1. Choose an informational topic, for example, "Puggles: A Hybrid Mix of the Beagle and the Pug."

2. Google the topic using a precise key term(s), for example, *puggle*.

3. For the first five sites that come up, answer these questions:

   • What information is contained on the site?

   • What is the nature of the information on the site? (Research- or fact-based, personal experience blog, persuasive/advertisement, and so on.)

   • In what situations would reading the information on this site help you? (For academic work, for personal enjoyment, and so on.)

   • What are the factors that help you judge the reliability of the information on the site? (Sources are referenced, few or no errors in grammar and spelling, recent publication for topics that change over time [e.g., technology], and so on.)

4. Select one of the five sites that provides information you think is credible and eligible to be included in a fact-based research paper for a school assignment. Compare with peers.

# Verifying Information

1. Choose an informational topic of your choice that is written about at Wikipedia.org.

2. Read the entire entry to get an overview of the topic.

3. Select one idea that is presented as fact.

4. Verify the fact by checking it against another source you judge to be reliable. (The References section at the end of the Wikipedia entry may or may not help.)

5. Compare with peers. Discuss these questions:

   • What source did you use to verify the fact?

   • How did you judge the credibility of the source you consulted?

6. Reflect on the need to verify sources by discussing these questions:

   • Why is it important to verify information found in various sources?

   • What criteria do you use to judge the credibility of sources?

   • In what ways have you found that authors "get things wrong"? (Misquoting? Overgeneralizing? Sensationalizing? Making typographical errors?)

# Avoiding Plagiarism

Plagiarism is the intentional or unintentional use of someone else's words without proper credit.

You need to give credit to:

- Ideas or words found in both print sources, such as books, magazines, and newspapers, and electronic sources, such as web pages and online informational texts, doing so by adding an in-text citation and including it in the references section.
- Words that you wish to use exactly as an author has used them, doing so by incorporating quotation marks, adding an in-text citation, and including it in the references section.
- Images and other media, such as diagrams, illustrations, photos, and audio/video, that you wish to enhance your text, doing so by incorporating a credit line within the text and including a citation in the references section.

Tips for avoiding plagiarism:

- Select sources that contain information that is written in easy-to-understand language.
- Use quotation marks in your notes when you use information exactly as it appears elsewhere.
- Paraphrase ideas when you can do so without losing the essence or intent of the ideas. Use "SOURCE:" or "According to ___" in your notes to help you wed your source with your paraphrase.
- Have a system for tracking your sources and/or compile your reference list as you go.

Read this information about puggles.

> Puggles are very sweet-tempered and playful. They are energetic, intelligent, and affectionate. A puggle is a great companion and will bond with you quickly. Puggles like to be in close contact and will follow you around the house. They are also very curious dogs that love to smell new things and find new places to go. They have a great sense of smell and will track scents like the beagle. Puggles are always happy to see you when you return from being away. A proud puggle will at times prance. To say a puggle is a social dog is an understatement. They love meeting new dogs at the dog parks or while out on a walk in the neighborhood.

"Puggle Breed Information." Puggle.org. Four Paws Enterprises, n.d. Web. 20 Dec. 2011.

1.  Write a sentence that *quotes* information from the source appropriately.

    Example:

    According to Puggle.org, puggles are "very curious dogs that love to smell new things and find new places to go" ("Puggle Breed Information").

    Your turn:

    _____

    _____

    _____

2.  Write a sentence that *paraphrases* information and credits the source appropriately.

    Example:

    A puggle gets a great sense of smell from its beagle parent ("Puggle Breed Information").

    Your turn:

    _____

    _____

3.  The following sentence is written in a way that is *not acceptable* according to plagiarism guidelines.

    A proud puggle will at times prance.

    Rewrite the sentence so that it is cited appropriately.

    _____

    _____

# Tracking Electronic and Print Sources

## Electronic

| Date of Retrieval | URL | Title of article/ information | Author information | Focus/Key points |
|---|---|---|---|---|
| 11/17/2012 | http://en.wikipedia.org /wiki/Puggle | "Puggle" | None given | History, description, health |
| | | | | |
| | | | | |
| | | | | |
| | | | | |
| | | | | |

## Print

| Title | Author | Publisher and Place of Publication | Copyright date | Focus/Key points |
|---|---|---|---|---|
| *Puggles: Everything About Purchase, Care, Nutrition, Behavior, and Training* | Andre Calbert | Hauppauge, NY: Barron's Educational Series. | 2007 | Purchasing a designer dog |
| | | | | |
| | | | | |
| | | | | |
| | | | | |

# Visual Nonfiction Essay Rubric: Research/Writing Aspects

Remember . . .

Visual: It is intended to be seen by viewers.
Nonfiction: It presents facts.
Essay: It is a short piece of writing on a particular subject.

| | Exemplary (3) | Proficient (2) | Minimally Proficient (1) | Unsatisfactory (0) |
|---|---|---|---|---|
| **Selection and Documentation of Sources** | Many credible print and electronic sources were consulted. | Multiple, mostly credible print and electronic sources were consulted. | Some sources appear credible, and more variety in sources was needed. | Sources, few in number, were not appropriate. |
| | All sources are properly documented. | Most sources are properly documented, although a few minor errors in citations may exist. | Some sources are improperly documented. | Documentation is absent. |
| **Storyboard** | Storyboard contains relevant text and image information and shows evidence of thought and decision making. | Storyboard contains mostly relevant text and image information and shows some evidence of thought and decision making. | Storyboard contains some irrelevant text and image information and may show insufficient thought and decision making. | Storyboard contains text and image information that is irrelevant, vague, or altogether missing and shows little thought and decision making. |
| **Content and Organization** | The content shows breadth and depth of ideas and is clearly connected to the purpose and theme. | Many ideas are conveyed well; the purpose and theme are evident. | Few ideas are presented and/ or some ideas are superficial. | Much of the information lacks cohesion in purpose, theme, and organization. |
| | The content is arranged logically. | The content is mostly arranged logically. | The arrangement of the content may be confusing at times. | |

# Visual Nonfiction Essay Rubric: Production Aspects

| | Exemplary (3) | Proficient (2) | Minimally Proficient (1) | Unsatisfactory (0) |
|---|---|---|---|---|
| **Graphic and Audio Appeal** | The essay has a finished, polished look; graphic elements are impactful and logical.<br><br>Audio is clear and enhances the message and mood. | The essay is appealing visually overall; graphic elements are mostly well placed and balanced.<br><br>Audio is usually an appropriate match for the content. | The essay contains some graphic interest, although some choices may not contribute to the meaning.<br><br>Audio may start and end abruptly or may distract from the message and mood at times. | The essay contains graphic elements that do not relate to the text or are more decorative than thoughtful.<br><br>Audio is missing, inappropriate, or overpowering. |
| **Transitions/Timing** | The essay flows seamlessly from one idea to the next at a reasonable pace. | The essay generally shows attention to pacing throughout without awkward transitions. | The essay contains some slack time, which distracts from the power and meaning. | The essay has many technical problems that hinders timing and detracts from the overall quality. |
| **Grammar and Mechanics** | The text contains no errors in grammar and mechanics. | The text contains a few errors in grammar and mechanics, but the errors are not overly distracting. | The text contains enough errors to be distracting from the meaning or message. | The text requires major editing because of the many errors in grammar and mechanics. |

# Topic Rationale and Blog Response Questions

Our topic is _____.

We selected this topic because _____

_____.

We plan to cover these major ideas: _____

_____.

We still have these questions: _____

_____

_____.

**Blog Response Questions**
- What aspect(s) about this topic appeals to you?
- Do you know of any resources this group can consult?
- Can you address or answer any of the group's questions?
- Do you have an idea that the group should consider?

*When Writing with Technology Matters* by Carol Bedard and Charles Fuhrken. Copyright © 2013. Stenhouse Publishers.

# Writing Words for Images

1. Find a photo with a cutline in a newspaper or magazine. (Most people refer to those explanatory words that appear underneath a photo a *caption*, but in the world of journalism they're called *cutlines*.)

2. Evaluate the cutline using the six criteria for creating a good cutline (see below). Make notes of which recommendations the writer of the cutline seemed to follow well and/or how the cutline might have been improved.

3. Compare with peers. Discuss how the art of writing cutlines relates to pairing text and images in a visual nonfiction essay.

---

**What Can We Learn from the Art of Cutline Writing?**

1. Know your audience.
   Keep in mind who you're writing the cutline for. What will your readers/viewers need and want to know?

2. Address what needs to be addressed.
   Think about the journalistic Ws—Who, What, When, Why, and Where—to guide you.

3. Just the facts!
   Stick to communicating the facts rather than inserting impressions about what someone might be thinking or feeling.

4. Avoid a "duh" moment.
   Leave out what is obvious. Viewer behavior is such that they look at the photo first before reading the words. So there's no need to explain what they can see for themselves (is obvious or a general impression) from looking at the photo. For a photo of a man in a white suit on a sunny day at a horse race, for instance, there is no need to include the details *white suit* and *sunny day* if the pertinent information is about the horse race.

5. Help with "busy" images.
   For those images with a lot of extra stuff in them, use clue/directional words to help viewers focus their attention (for example, "the captain [*right*]").

6. Write tight!
   Reread and revise to remove the "clutter"—any information that detracts from the image rather than enhances it. Use the fewest words to communicate the gist.

---

# Evaluating Media Messages

1. Choose an electronic source for information such as britannica.com or an online magazine or an online newspaper that is free or to which the school has a subscription.

2. Find a text that uses both images (for example, photos, illustrations) and words (for example, captions or cutlines, an informational article) to communicate the message or meaning. (For example, on the home page of britannica.com, you will likely see an "On This Day" or "Born This Day" feature that shows an image and displays a short bit of text.)

3. Evaluate the effectiveness of the image by addressing these questions:

    • How many distinct ideas do the words communicate (for example, one, two, many) and what are they?

    • How are the words included with an image like a main idea or summary?

    • What is the nature of the information communicated with the words (for example, facts, opinions, quotations from experts)?

    • How and why is the image suited to the words?

    • What is the intended impact of the words and image on the reader/viewer?

    • What would be lost if either the words or the image were not there?

    • What are important considerations when pairing words and images to communicate messages and meaning?

4. Compare with peers the information sources and your answers to these questions.

# References

## Professional Literature

Avgerinou, Maria. n.d. "What Is 'Visual Literacy'?" International Visual Literacy Association. http://www.ivla.org/org_what_vis_lit.htm.

Blumenfeld, P. C., E. Soloway, R. W. Marx, J. S. Krajcik, M. Guzdial, and A. Palincsar. 1991. "Motivating Project-Based Learning: Sustaining the Doing, Supporting the Learning." *Educational Psychologist* 26 (3): 369–398.

Bruce, B. C. 1997. "Literacy Technologies: What Stance Should We Take?" *Journal of Literacy Research* 29 (2): 289–309.

Buckingham, D. 2003. *Media Education: Literacy, Learning, and Contemporary Culture.* Hoboken, NJ: John Wiley and Sons.

Cambourne, B. 1989. Theory into Practice. *The Whole Story.* Gosford, New South Wales, Australia: Ashton Scholastic.

Clinton, W. J. 1997. "President Clinton's Call to Action for American Education in the 21st Century: Technological Literacy" (pp. 39–42). http://www.clintonlibrary.gov/assets/storage/Research%20-%20Digital%20Library/Reed-Education/94/647429-sotu.pdf.

Cohen, V. L., and J. E. Cowen. 2008. *Literacy for Children in an Information Age: Teaching Reading, Writing, and Thinking.* Belmont, CA: Thomson Higher Education.

Essley, R., L. Rief, and A. L. Rocci. 2008. *Visual Tools for Differentiating Reading and Writing Instruction: Strategies to Help Students Make Abstract Ideas Concrete and Accessible.* New York: Scholastic.

Goodman, S. 2003. *Teaching Youth Media: A Critical Guide to Literacy, Video Production, and Social Change.* New York: Teachers College.

Hobbs, R. 2007. *Reading the Media: Media Literacy in High School English.* New York: Teachers College.

Jonassen, D. H., K. L. Peck, and B. G. Wilson. 1999. *Learning with Technology: A Constructivist Perspective.* Columbus, OH: Prentice Hall.

Kajder, S. 2010. *Adolescents and Digital Literacies: Learning Alongside Our Students.* Urbana, IL: National Council of Teachers of English.

Kristeva, J. 1984. *Revolution in Poetic Language.* New York: Columbia University Press.

Leu, D. 1997. "Caity's Question: Literacy as Deixis on the Internet." *The Reading Teacher* 51 (1): 62–67.

Messaris, P. 1994. *Visual Literacy: Image, Mind and Reality.* Boulder, CO: Westview Press.

Ong, W. 2002. *Orality and Literacy: The Technologizing of the Word.* London, England: Routledge.

Partnership for 21st Century Skills. 2011. "Our Mission: P21 Mission Statement." Washington, DC: Partnership for 21st Century Skills. http://www.p21.org/about-us/our-mission.

Prensky, M. 2001. "Digital Natives, Digital Immigrant." *On the Horizon*. West Yorkshire, UK: MCB University Press.

Smolin, L. I., and K. A. Lawless. 2003. "Becoming Literate in the Technological Age: New Responsibilities and Tools for Teachers." *The Reading Teacher* 56 (6): 570–577.

Strassman, B. K., and T. O'Connell. 2007–2008. "Authoring with Video." *The Reading Teacher* 61 (4): 330–333.

Swed, J. F. 2001. "The Ethnography of Literacy." In *Literacy: A Critical Sourcebook*, ed. E. Cushman, E. R. Kintgen, B. M. Kroll, and M. Rose, 421–429. Boston, MA: Bedford/St. Martin's.

Vannatta, R. A., and N. Fordham. 2004. "Teacher Dispositions as Predictors of Classroom Technology Use." *Journal of Research on Technology in Education* 36 (3): 253–271.

# Children's and Young Adult Literature

Abbott, T. 2007. *Firegirl*. New York: Little, Brown.

Benton, J. 2004. *Dear Dumb Diary: My Pants Are Haunted*. New York: Scholastic.

Blackwood, G. 2000. *Shakespeare Stealer*. New York: Penguin.

Boniface, W. 2006. *The Extraordinary Adventures of Ordinary Boy: The Hero Revealed*. New York: HarperCollins.

Campbell, G. 2009. *The Boys' Book of Survival: How to Survive Anything, Anywhere*. New York: Scholastic.

Clements, A. 1996. *Frindle*. New York: Simon and Schuster Books for Young Readers.

———. 2005. *Lunch Money*. New York: Simon and Schuster Books for Young Readers.

Collier, J. L., and C. Collier. 1974. *My Brother Sam Is Dead*. New York: Scholastic.

Collins, S. 2003. *Gregor the Overlander*. New York: Scholastic.

———. 2010. *The Hunger Games*. New York: Scholastic.

Coville, B. 1989. *My Teacher Is an Alien*. New York: Aladdin.

Cullen, L. 2007. *I Am Rembrandt's Daughter*. New York: Bloomsbury.

Curtis, C. P. 2000. *The Watsons Go to Birmingham—1963*. New York: Random House.

Farmer, N. 2006. *The Sea of Trolls*. New York: Simon & Schuster.

Grant, K. M. 2004. *Blood Red Horse*. New York: Walker & Company.

Haddix, M. P. 2007. *Dexter the Tough*. New York: Aladdin.

Hesse, K. 1997. *Out of the Dust*. New York: Scholastic.

Konigsburg, E. L. 1975. *The Second Mrs. Gioconda*. New York: Simon & Schuster.

Napoli, D. J. 2007. *Hush: An Irish Princess Tale*. New York: Atheneum.

Paterson, K. 1977. *Bridge to Terabithia*. New York: HarperCollins.

Preus, M. 2011. *Heart of a Samurai*. New York: Abrams.

Riordan, R. 2009. *The Lightning Thief*. New York: Hyperion.

Ryan, P. M. 2002. *Esperanza Rising*. New York: Scholastic.

Scieszka, J. 1989. *The True Story of the 3 Little Pigs!* New York: Puffin.

Soto, G. 2003. *Taking Sides*. Boston, MA: Houghton Mifflin Harcourt.

Spinelli, J. 1992. *Report to the Principal's Office*. New York: Scholastic.

Stevens, J. 1995. *Tops and Bottoms*. New York: Houghton Mifflin Harcourt.

West, T., and K. Noll. 2008. *Aly and AJ's Rock-n-Roll Mysteries: First Stop, New York*. New York: Penguin.

Woodson, J. 2010. *After Tupac and D Foster*. New York: Penguin.

## Film

Csupo, G. 2007. *Bridge to Terabithia*. DVD recording. Walt Disney Pictures and Walden Media.

# Index

Page numbers followed by an *f* indicate figures.

# R

# S

# DATE DUE

PRINTED IN U.S.A.